THE ANCIENT WAYS OF ...

Also by Richard Sale

A Guide to the Cotswold Way
A Visitor's Guide to the Cotswolds
A Walker's Guide to Europe
   (with Arthur Howcroft)
A Cambrian Way
The Wye Valley
Dorset
Owain Glyndwr's Way

Richard Sale and Arthur Lees

THE ANCIENT WAYS OF LAKELAND

A circular route for walkers

 *André Deutsch*

First published 1986
by André Deutsch Limited
105 Great Russell Street London WC1

Photographs by the authors

ISBN 0 233 97799 6

CONTENTS

INTRODUCTION

"The Country although it be somewhat of the coldest as lying farre north, and seemeth as rough by reason of hilles, yet for the variety thereof it smileth upon the beholders and giveth contentment to as many as travaile it. For after the rockes bunching out, the mountains standing thicke together, rich of metall mines, and between them great meeres stored with all kindes of wildfowle, you come to pretty hilles good for pasturage, and well replenished with flocks of sheepe, beneath which again you meet with goodly plaines, spreading out a great way, yielding corn sufficiently. Beside all this the ocean driving and dashing upon the shore affourdeth plenty of excellent good fish."

In this way the Elizabethan traveller Camden described Cumberland, which includes the area that is covered by this book. The accurate Camden was one of the first to visit the area as a tourist, but there have been many who have travelled in his footsteps. They came for a variety of reasons: because it is beautiful and because it has much to offer to the naturalist, the historian, the industrial archaeologist, and many more.

There have been many books on walking the Lakeland fells, but these invariably concentrate on routes to the tops. This is not surprising – Lakeland has the highest summits in England and there are many who wish to walk that highest ground. But at a lower level there is much that is of interest.

The high fells slope outwards from a central raised dome, a series of deep valleys radiating out from the centre. The valleys hold the lakes, looking, from the air, like the spokes of a wheel with its hub near Langdale. A circular route enters all the valleys, visiting all the lakes, but such a route needs to cross the ridges that define the valleys. It is here that our book differs from all others, for we chose to cross the ridges not at their highest points, but at their lowest, at the passes that represent the ancient ways from valley to valley.

We have chosen to use the ancient ways because we seek not only the scenery of Lakeland, but its history, factual and legendary. Lakeland is a fascinating place. The Scots and the Welsh were able to maintain an independence from the stream of invaders who ravaged England, the former because of their remoteness, the latter because of the mountains of Snowdon and the granary of Anglesey. Not so Lakeland whose accessibility allowed a procession of inhabitants each bringing their own language and culture. While this means that the area's history is fragmented, it also means that the folk-legend net is cast over a wider sea.

Our search for Lakeland's history will encompass its industrial heritage as well as its folk heritage, and for that too we must keep to the lower slopes. And it is in the history of the exploitation of the area's natural resources that we find other reasons for its scenery. In these days of increasing concern over the conservation of the National Park it is interesting to note that once Coniston Water was poisoned by the waste from the local copper mines.

What we offer in this book is a tour of Lakeland that visits all the lakes, crossing the passes between them. The outlying lakes of Bassenthwaite, and Loweswater are visited by out-and-back routes, and the central lakes of Grasmere, Rydal Water and Elterwater are visited in a short round trip. The complete round tour is about 120 miles, but obviously it is not necessary to walk it in one outing.

Sticks Pass

Lakeland should be savoured, not taken by storm. To assist this the circular walk is given in short lake-to-lake sections, each one having a return route to the start point, so that the full route can be accomplished as a series of small round trips or any one of the sections can be walked on its own. These round trips are of day length, ranging from about 6 miles up to about 15 miles.

Many of the passes we will cross have been highways for centuries, and we will be following in the footsteps of some famous people, as well as of generations of ordinary lakelanders. The Wordsworths, perhaps Lakeland's most famous residents, were great walkers, finding their daffodils on foot. William Wordsworth composed as he walked, and since he did his walking dressed in a style that would be roundly condemned by just about every outdoor pursuit body today, it is, perhaps, small surprise to discover that he died as a result of walking in cold winter rain without a hat. Of course he *was* eighty! Wordsworth knew, and those who follow our journey through Lakeland will find, that Camden was right – "it giveth contentment to as many as travaile it".

THE BACKGROUND

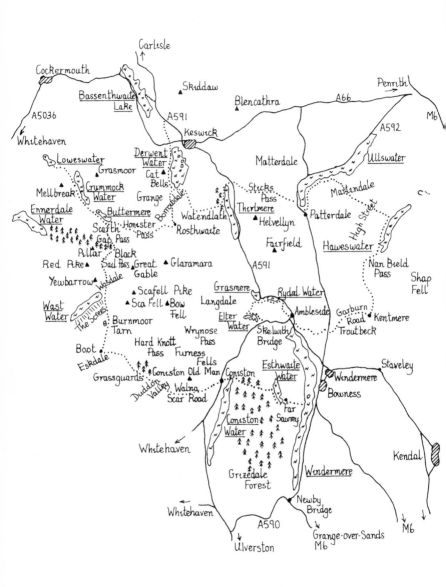

GEOLOGY AND GEOGRAPHY

Lakeland is composed primarily of three bands of ancient rocks running from the south-west to the north-east. In theory this should produce a straightforward variation in the scenery as we move from the south northwards, and indeed it does. But so complex has been the building and erosion of mountains, the faulting of the underlying rock structure and the effects of glaciation that within the basic framework there is a series of local geologies and, therefore, local environments.

The oldest Lakeland rock is the Skiddaw Slate of the geological era known as the Ordovician. The rock is fine-grained and dark, a sedimentary rock laid down as mud beneath shallow, still waters some 500 million years ago. Pressure and temperature compressed, hardened and cleaved the original mudstones, capturing and preserving at the same time some of the marine creatures. Of these, trilobites are perhaps the best known, though the rock is hardly a happy hunting ground for the fossil-hunter. Neither is it a particularly useful rock for the slater, despite its name, the cleavage being poor. The Skiddaw Slates lie north of a line that, roughly, joins Ennerdale Water to Derwent Water, and so includes not only Skiddaw itself, but the Buttermere to Loweswater Valley. Within that area there are rock outcrops, mainly due to later intrusions of hard, sharp igneous rocks, but the overall impression of the slates country is of smooth-sided rolling fells.

The Honister Pass allows us to view, at first hand, the dramatic change that occurred in Lakeland around 470 million years ago. From the head of the pass the slates country lies to our right, the (relatively) easy angled, vegetated slopes leading off to smooth fell. To our left there are the sharp, steep cliffs of Honister Crag. This is an outcrop of the Borrowdale Volcanic Series. The volcanic activity was the result of plate movements in the earth's crust caused by deep convectional currents. The igneous rocks produced are between eight and twelve thousand feet thick and occupy the majority of central Lakeland. To deposit such a depth of material over so wide an area, the volcanic activity of the area must have persisted for some considerable time; several million years, it is believed. There are no old volcanoes now in Lakeland, though Castle Head Crag, near Keswick, is believed to be a plug in an ancient volcanic vent.

The Borrowdale Volcanic Series rocks, the "ejectments shot or poured out from volcanoes" as one geologist from the first decade of this century had it, are hard, fine-grained rocks, pressure-converted to slates, the famous ornamental green slate of Lakeland. These rocks are responsible for the angular scenery of the central dome of the National Park, extending southward from the Skiddaw Slates to a line that, roughly, connects Coniston and Ambleside but extends beyond each of them.

As the volcanoes become extinct, the rocks were uplifted and folded into a mountainous mass, and remained in this state for several million years during which erosion worked away at the upper rocks, rounding off the rough edges and lowering the hills.

The sea then returned: a clear sea below which the Coniston Limestone was laid down to a depth of 1000 feet. Of this only a strip now remains, a fence separating the hard volcanic land to the north from the Silurian land to the south. The fence, obviously, runs along the border given above for the Borrowdale Series. The Silurian rocks to the south of the Coniston Limestone were also laid down below a sea that covered Lakeland, though here the sea was muddier and of varying depth, giving rise to a larger number of rock types; slates and shales, grits and flags. The overall scenery is low and gentle, but with occasional knobbly bits.

At the end of the Silurian era, some 400 million years ago, the main rock components of present-day Lakeland were in existence. Then the rocks of Lakeland were lifted up by the first of three mountain-building phases which have given us the area's underlying structure. The first phase of orogeny, or mountain building, is known as the Caledonian because it was largely responsible for the production of the mountains of Scotland. During this time the hard granite rocks that cause such locally exciting scenery were squeezed into fault lines in the main rocks. There are many such intrusions, the most famous, perhaps, being Shap granite which has been extensively quarried. Our route will pass Eskdale granite, a rough rock, pink from haematite and used in wall-building, and Ennerdale granophyre, another hard, pink rock.

The Lakeland mountains caused by the upheaval were of Hima-layan proportions, but though mountains may seem eternal to most of us, to the geologist they most certainly are not, and about 350 million years ago the area was once more beneath the sea. This time the sea was clear and calm, filled with coral and crinoids, and the rock that was laid down below it is a fossil-based rock, carboniferous limestone.

As the seas receded forests took root in the marginal swamp area, becoming in their turn the coal measures that lie below the coastal limestone belt.

The Carboniferous period lasted for about 80 million years and at the end of this time a second period of mountain building commenced. The earth movement of the "Hercynian orogeny" was less violent than its forerunner, though its effect was to accentuate aspects of the Caledonian upheaval some 120 million years before. Much of the mineral wealth of the area developed during this period: the haemetite seams in the west are thought to be older.

With the rocks again above water the carboniferous limestone was eroded away, so that today there is none in the upland central area, though it comprises the majority of the surrounding lowland belt.

The familiar cycle repeated itself once again with sea encroachment and the deposition of rock ending in a third mountain building phase about sixty million years ago. This time the centre of activity was around the Scafell area. The same sequence of earth movements was responsible for the Alps, and the "Alpine orogeny" left the Lakeland fells at about their present size. In addition, though later agencies were also important, this phase of mountain building, by creating a central high rocky dome, produced the radial drainage pattern that gave rise to the spokes-of-a-wheel valleys so characteristic of Lakeland.

The above description of the underlying geology of Lakeland goes some way to explaining the differences that can occur within a very few miles, but it is not a sufficient explanation of the geography of the area. It was not the volcanoes and geological upheavals of millions of years ago, which must be measured by a timescale on which man is an upstart, that gave Lakeland the shape we know. It was finally sculpted and moulded by the Ice Ages, forces that occurred as little as 15,000 years ago, when man was much as he is today. When the ice moved south Lakeland became a polar desert. At the extreme of glaciation the ice was 2,000 feet thick, probably filling the deepest valleys to form a continuous ice cap over the entire area. Certainly there are icy remnants at a high level – glacial scourings on Scafell at 2,500 feet, glacial erratics on High Stile above Buttermere. The centre of the high ice plateau was around Esk Hause, from where glaciers radiated outward. Those flowing north met Scottish ice flowing south. The two ice masses coalesced, moving west then south down what is now the Irish Sea, or east through the Tyne gap, or east and south down the Eden Vale. The glaciers that headed west and east met those that had gone north, only the south-flowing ice having free passage, out into Morecombe Bay.

Moving ice corrodes. It abrades the surfaces over which it passes, tearing out lumps of rocks, eating its way downwards and back towards its head. To see at first hand the effect of such movements, stand near the top of Helvellyn, a point a little removed from our route, and note the extreme difference between the western side of the mountain with its virtually pre-glacial form – a long, easy-angled grassy slope – and the eastern side with its sheer, rugged cliffs. The underlying rock is the same, but on the east flank it has been torn into cragginess. This tearing also produced the crags around Scafell.

Also on this eastern flank of Helvellyn is another feature of glaciation. As the glaciers eat back towards their heads they form the "armchair-shaped" hollows so familiar to walkers, and known as "cirques" to the geographer. The word *cirque* is French, and there are many local names for the features. In Wales they are *cwms* – a name transferred to the western side of Everest by an early climber familiar with Wales; in Scotland they are corries. In Lakeland they are coves, from *cofa*, Old English for hollow. There are coves on Helvellyn, as elsewhere. What is different here is that two coves have been produced back to back, as it were, the ridge of rock between them having been steepened and thinned to form an arête. Such arêtes are another well-known glacial feature, though they are rare in Lakeland where the glaciation was intense, ironing out some of the extremes of geography. Striding Edge on Helvellyn's east flank is a good arête, and so is Riggindale Crag below High Street, that our route will pass.

Within the coves the rock was scoured and its rubble was pushed forward by the glacier. As the climate improved and the glaciers melted and shrank, some of this "moraine" was left beyond the deepest rock basins, sealing them off from the lower slopes. In such basins water was caught, producing tarns, those most beautiful of

Lakeland waters. A very fine example, Small Water, below the Nan Bield Pass, is passed by our route.

Such over-deepening of the ground below the glaciers is also seen in the main glacial valleys, and this effect caused the creation of hanging valleys in many tributaries to the main valleys. Here the side

Small water and Haweswater from Nan Bield Pass

valley is less deepened, a rock step being produced between its mouth and the main valley floor. At these rock steps the forces, or waterfalls, of Lakeland were produced: before the Ice Ages there would have been few, if any, waterfalls. Our route passes many of these fine glacial cataracts, Lodore Falls from the Watendlath valley into Borrowdale being perhaps the most famous.

Not all of the area's waterfalls were produced in this way. Some occur where hard rock butts onto soft rock. Here the glacial effect is not constant, the soft rock eroding faster than the hard to form a sill. Usually such falls are not as high, and at a shallower angle, but they can still be very picturesque, as Skelwith Force on our route shows.

Another effect of glaciation is the creation of mounds of moraine at odd points in the area. One fine example of such oddness is the formation of the "Ees" spurs in Esthwaite Water, lumps of land thrust into the lake that give it such an appealing shape.

The final effect of the Ice Ages that cannot be overlooked is the interference in the natural drainage pattern brought about by the glaciers. The ice, radiating out from Esk Hause, accentuated the radial valley development, overdeepening the spokes-of-a-wheel valleys. Within the over-deepened spokes lakes were formed. The Ice Age had created Lakeland.

And here we had better explain the difference between a tarn and a lake. Each is defined by the most common of its emergent plants. In a tarn it is the bottle sedge, in a lake it is the common reed. Thus, though Burnmoor Tarn and Loweswater are comparable in size, the former is a tarn and the latter is a lake. Similarly, little Brotherswater is a lake (which, since it is not included on our list, is somewhat embarrassing!). And, while we are on the subject of water, when is a tarn not a pond? Boo Tarn, beside our route as we follow the Walna Scar road is, after all, only a splash of water. It has an outflow, however, and it is that which makes it a tarn. Only static water can be a pond.

On a geological time scale there is no reason to suppose that the process of evolution has ceased, but our present concern should be that man should not introduce changes on a far shorter time scale. In the past forty years, with increased ease of transport and leisure time, the number of people visiting Lakeland has dramatically increased. This clearly puts a considerable burden on the National Park authorities in guarding against fellside erosion. There has been re-routing of some footpaths, and the insertion of artificial steps to protect the slopes. To the purist, these intrusions are unwelcome, but if by modifying the busiest paths in this way, it is possible to enable large numbers of people to enjoy this unique part of the countryside without hastening its decline, it is a small price to pay.

About 12,000 years ago, as the Lakeland climate began to warm up, plants invaded the area. First came juniper and willow, then birch, the tree cover eventually reaching 2,500 feet. Now, much of that tree cover is gone, or has been replaced by the alien conifer. Some was used for charcoal to supply heat to the budding iron industry, but much was lost due to the activities of that apparently most innocuous of nibblers, the sheep.

The renowned Lakeland sheep is the Herdwick, which Beatrix

Potter used to breed, but which now comprises, in pure-bred form, a very small percentage of all the area's sheep. There is dispute about the origin of the Herdwick. Some say it swam ashore from the wreck of a Spanish Armada galleon lost in a storm of Muncaster – and if that is true, then the Armada was in part successful, landing a small army from Spain to devastate one corner of England. Some say it is Norse in origin, pointing to the Viking content of the Lakeland shepherds' special dialect.

It is a short stocky animal, very tough, and had a reputation for going both upward and windward on its hill if a storm approached. The theory was that the sheep was clever enough to position itself so that it would not be overblown. In fact this story, traceable (in print, at least) to 1787, has no foundation, and the Herdwick behaves exactly like any other sheep. But it is a good survivor, nibbling at the heather tops when snow has fallen through the ling.

The sheep were tended by shepherds who knew both their fells and their animals. There is even historical evidence for the trepanning of sheep to remove the cysts of toxicara worms to prevent blindness. (Only now are we awakening to the unpleasantness of those worms and starting to keep dogs out of children's sand-pits.) The lowland farmers with their cows were probably just as caring of their animals, but occasionally a darker side to the pastoral life emerged. If too many bull calves were born, or there were too many abortions, a calf was burnt alive. This, and a later remedy where the cows were passed through the smoke of a fire, seem to be remnants of Baal sacrifice and Beltane fires. There are those who see the "Bell" of Cat Bells as deriving not from Bield, but from Baal. The country near Burnmoor Tarn is an ancient landscape. Beware the fell mists, they might be the smoke from something sinister . . .

But we have digressed from Lakeland geography, even if farming, along with tourism of course, is now the major influence on it. Within the remnants of the ancient landscape, barren or afforested, the Lakeland flora and fauna cling on. There are red deer in the remaining Furness Fell woods, and in Martindale, on our route. There are red squirrels and, though much rarer, pine martens. There are foxes still, though hunting appears to have eliminated the large, grey, long-legged fell foxes that gave "sport" for six hours or more. The usual crop of moorland birds has now been augmented by England's only golden eagles – Long may they thrive! And Lakeland is home to Britain's only alpine butterfly, the Mountain Ringlet whose caterpillars eat grass.

Among the "original" forest left by the charcoal-burners and the sheep are Glencoyne Wood and the trees on Hallin Fell, both near Ullswater and our route. Another relic is Johnny's Wood in Borrowdale, through which we shall walk. Here the trees are stunted in comparison to their lowland English cousins, but superb for all that.

Lakeland is wet and windy. Seathwaite, at the head of Borrowdale, has the dubious distinction of being the wettest place in England. There it rains, on average, on 236 days each year, and collects 131 inches of rain. Less famous, but in fact wetter, is Sprinkling Tarn, a couple of miles to the south, where the annual average rainfall is believed to be 185 inches.

While Sprinkling Tarn is the extreme, the rainfall of the upland heart of Lakeland is high everywhere. This is fine for reservoirs, but it is not the best weather for tourists. But all is not lost, and by a strange quirk of climate, it is the wind – not usually the best-loved of nature's elements – that comes to the visitor's rescue. Lakeland has "helm" winds which have a strong drying effect and can cause long periods of rain-free days. To reduce the chances of rain, visit the area from March to June, when the wind is most likely to blow.

In fact the Lakeland climate, with its mild, windy winters and cool, cloudy summers, while giving the impression that the English weather is rotten, is one to boast of when you consider that Lakeland is at the same latitude as Moscow. It is only the presence of the warm ocean beside it that maintains the climate at such a mild level. Despite the mildness, however, the late springs, cool summers and the wind mean that the tree limit is very low on the fell-side. To compensate, the high latitude means great changes in light intensity, which gives the area those tonal qualities that have long attracted the artist. Lakeland is a very special place in which to look at things: to learn how true this is, look at the same view at different times of day and in different seasons.

The mountains, of course, produce their own weather, and often conditions on the fell will be very different from those in the valleys. They may even vary from fell to fell. The "bottom" winds of Derwent Water are good examples of this very local weather. The Honister Pass has "the Crack", a wind that reputedly can blow turnips out of the ground (it has also been known to lift people off the ridge and throw them down Honister Crag, which is altogether less amusing). And Lakeland has many stories of thunderstorms following hot days that have produced huge rises in beck levels with devastating local results.

It is in winter, however, that the mountain weather is to be taken most seriously. The ever-present wind – it really does blow more frequently and harder here than in other parts of England – turns a cold day into a raw and dangerous one. Please do take the hills seriously.

HISTORY

The ice ages obliterated all trace of whatever earlier inhabitants there may have been in the Lakeland fells. Only when the climate had warmed did man leave his first mark.

8,000 years ago, when the Mesolithic, or Middle Stone Age, hunter-gatherers arrived, the uplands were afforested. Though capable of producing from a flint an edge for cutting meat and scraping skins, and of carving a primitive but adequate harpoon from bone, these early settlers were far from commanding the technology to clear the forests. They kept instead to the coast where the sea was a well-stocked larder and they could hunt in the sparser forests on the inland side of the shore-line dunes. The beaches were littered with flint nodules deposited by the glaciers, and the working of these left small fragments, known as microliths, which serve as the first direct evidence of habitation. Microliths have been found at St Bees Head, while on a raised beach at Eskmeals, on the southern side of the Esk estuary, there is evidence of extensive working. There may even have been an industry. And on the other side of the estuary, at Drigg to the north of Ravenglass, there is, perhaps, evidence of another, similar prehistoric industrial site. Drigg is now a dump for debris from Britain's nuclear power programme, that most modern of industries.

The painstaking accumulation of evidence such as microliths is just one of the aspects of modern archaeology. Equally fascinating is the use of an analysis of pollen laid down over centuries from surrounding vegetation to investigate changes in that vegetation and hence in land usage. Dr Donald Walker, working at Ehenside Tarn, near Beckermet to the south of Egremont, has found that the local vegetation was modified about 6,000 years ago, and conjectures that this might have been due to deliberate firing of the forest in order to produce a clearing around a mesolithic camp.

Further pollen analysis shows that around 5,000 years ago Lakeland became ready for the farming which began to be practised by settlers of the Neolithic, or New Stone Age. The elm tree pollen count falls – the trees were felled, their leaves were fed to domestic, stock animals; the grass pollen increases and cereal pollen occurs for the first time. These beginnings of farming followed the production of better stone implements. The polished stone axe was an impressive tool. It could be hafted to clear forests in a more controlled way than by burning (perhaps the resulting timber was used for housing), and it could be used as a plough, harrow and hoe to cultivate the clearing. The production of the axes was also an industry. The chief industrial site has been found on the scree slopes below Pike of Stickle in Langdale. It was not flint that was worked here – the scarcity of that prized rock calling for a substitute. The fine-grained ash of the Borrowdale Volcanic Series (green Langdale harstone) allowed production of an axe of high-quality, the rough tool being produced at source and transported to the "village" sites, or perhaps to specific coastal sites, for polishing with sharp sand. So good were the Lakeland axes that they were bartered as far afield as Scotland, the Isle of Man and Ireland.

As farming developed, so a more settled way of life began, with more time available for activities additional to those required just to stay alive. In other areas throughout Britain this led to the first permanent monuments to man's existence, the long barrows. In Lakeland, however, such burial mounds are rarely found, perhaps because the intensive cultivation of the coastal strip has eroded the barrows. The earliest permanent monuments in the area derive from the Bronze Age, when the transition from stone to metal cultures took place with the coming of the Beaker folk. These monuments are the megaliths (from the Greek, "great stones") – the standing stones and stone circles. The Beaker folk are named from a particular form of pottery they used, which is often found in their burial mounds, the round barrows. They are famous for their presumed association with Stonehenge and other henge sites.

The largest of the sites is that known as Long Meg and her Daughters, about seven miles to the north-east of Penrith, which has an oval measuring 120 yards by 100 yards of some sixty stones, many ten feet tall. These stones are the Daughters. Long Meg is a twelve-foot menhir (that is, standing stone) twenty yards away from the oval. The stones have not only been raised but dressed, and Meg herself is decorated with incised "cup and ring" marks. Authoritative opinion rates this site second only to Stanton Drew, south of Bristol, in order of importance among the "lesser" British megalithic circles. (Both these circles are, of course, rated lower than Stonehenge itself, and than Avebury.)

But if Long Meg and her Daughters is the most important Lakeland site in the archaeological sense, then Castlerigg, a little way east of Keswick, is the most dramatic. Viewed from any direction it has an impressive backdrop of high fell, and when the site is empty, as it usually is, and cloud hugs the landscape, it is an evocative place. Castlerigg is visited by one of the routes described in the book.

Castlerigg

For those interested in megalithic sites Lakeland is a good hunting ground, because the stones frequently stand on open fell, with a surrounding area largely untouched since the time of erection. The circle at (060 140) on Beakley Moss near Severnside is just such a site. A notable exception to this rule is the circle at Greycroft from which the Sellafields nuclear complex can be viewed.

The magnetism of such sites is undeniable – a mixture of mystery because the reasons for their erection are not well understood, and majesty. The labour involved in dressing and raising the stones was considerable. Recently such sites have attracted considerable "earth-magic" interest and it is not unusual to read of them as markers for intergalactic travel, and as battery terminals for positive (or negative!) energy. It is known that some sites are astronomically aligned, chiefly against the rising or setting of the sun, though the significance even of this is disputed. They must have been used for some ritual purpose: that is all that it is possible to say. And it is just that vagueness, of course, that allows myth-building.

Many of the burial sites from this period, like the stone circles, are on the fells: but this does not suggest that Bronze Age people were specially hardy. There is evidence that the climate was warmer and more settled than it is today. The seas were therefore less of a barrier to the "primitive" Lakelanders than one might expect, and there is evidence of significant trade with Ireland and the Isle of Man. However there was a shift towards a colder, wetter and consequently stormy climate some 2,500 years ago, which reduced sea-trading and also made life in Lakeland harsher. Consequently the area became depopulated, with a gradual re-establishment of the original vegetation. It was at this time that Britain was first being settled by iron-users from continental Europe. The early iron-users were from central and eastern Europe, their cultures being termed first Hallstatt, then La Tène, from villages in Austria and Switzerland respectively. The popular name for the peoples derives from that given by the Romans to the inhabitants of Gaul, now France. Though often referred to as the Galli, they were also termed Keltoi, giving us our word "Celt". The iron-using Celts brought with them mixed farming, improved craft techniques and the horse. One of the few finds from Celtic Lakeland is a bronze bit with red enamel decoration from Place Fell, Ullswater, dated to the first century AD.

Elsewhere in Britain the most obvious imprint of the Celtic tribes on the landscape is the hill-fort. Early forms of these were hilltops, or promontories, whose natural defences were enhanced by the construction of a single ditch and rampart. Later, as an answer to the sling-shot whose range in skilled hands was prodigious, multiple rows of ditches and ramparts were produced. Lakeland has nothing that even remotely approaches the scale of Maiden Castle in Dorset, which could shelter about 4000 people. Hill-forts do exist, but they are small and very few. The most impressive is on Carrock Fell, north of Blencathra, but even that is limited to only five acres. It is thought probable that this fort was the headquarters in Lakeland of the Brigatines, the Celtic tribe who occupied northern England when yet another new culture arrived from mainland Europe. This time, unlike the earlier comers who seem to have been absorbed peaceably, the new culture was imposed at the point of a sword – the Roman short sword.

The Romans invaded Britain in earnest in 43AD and moved quickly through their new realm, defeating those Celtic tribes who resisted and setting up governorships in those that acquiesced. By 47AD the state of Brigantia, the most populous of British states according to Tacitus, existed in northern England. We cannot know of the true feelings of the Brigantes towards the occupation, however generous its terms, but the existence of a military front to the north probably meant that the Romans were nervous and reacted immediately to any dissension. Brigantia was ruled by Venutius who was not enamoured of the Romans. His queen Cartimandua, on the other hand, was pro-Roman, to the extent that in 51AD she handed over to them Caratacus, the British leader who had fought them first in southern England and then in Wales before seeking sanctuary in the north.

The Brigantines did revolt eventually to be crushed by the Romans under Petillius Cerialis. In the wake of this action Lakeland itself saw the first true occupation with the construction of roads and forts. Initially the roads skirted the upland centre, going northward from Penrith to Carlisle, and across the coastal strip route of the Solway Firth. Only later were the forts of Galava, at Ambleside, and Mediobogdum (Hard Knott) built, together with the High Street road. A stone found at the Hard Knott fort tells that it was constructed around 120AD, for the Emperor Caesar Trajan Hadrian Augustus, by troops from Dalmatia (now part of Yugoslavia). The Emperor is less famous for the construction of this fort than for the wall built in his name that extends from the Solway Firth to the Tyne. (Hadrian's Wall lies well north of our area, but should by no means be missed by anyone interested in the Roman period of British history.)

Given that the Ambleside and Hard Knott forts were built in the first quarter of the second century, the question is; why? By then the Brigantines were subdued and Hadrian's Wall had eliminated incursions by the "barbarians", as Hadrian's biographer Aurelius Victor has it, to the north. The road from Ambleside, on which the Hard Knott fort was just a staging post, went to the coast at Ravenglass where there was a fortified port, Glannaventa. The fortifications were not seaward, however, so the road did not exist to protect the north of Roman Britain from seaborne invasion. There are two other possible interpretations. One is that Ravenglass received supplies for this most north-western corner of the Empire, and the road to Ambleside and the Wall was fortified as a precaution against the supply route, or supply trains, being attacked by renegade Brigantines (skirmishes with the native Celts almost certainly did not stop with the crushing of the revolt, only fifty years before). The other possibility is that the Romans were preparing for an invasion of Ireland. This theory seemed to make sense when the Ambleside fort was still believed to have been constructed by Agricola, because there is evidence to suggest that he believed that Ireland was half way between England and Spain, which would have made its invasion attractive. But now that it is known that the fort is of a much later date, evidence to support the invasion theory seems less well-founded.

The Galava site is hardly a great tourist attraction. There is little to see. The fort stood in a field now called "Borrans", a Norse word for a heap of stones – all that remained when the Norsemen arrived here half a millenium after the Romans had departed. In such habitable areas ruins frequently became quarries, and the heap of stones would have been fast depleted. Excavations have shown that the first fort was of timber and earth, but later it was of stone with a granary and barracks for 500 men. To the fortifications were added the protection of the River Rothay, which at that time flowed closer to the Borrans field. The surrounding natives were not always so threatening, because eventually a small Romanised settlement grew up outside the fort.

The Roman fort of Mediobogdum, at Hard Knott, is a sharp contrast to the Galava site. The Roman name translates as the "fort in the middle of the curve", an apt description for the position below the Hard Knott pass, but hardly capturing the awe-inspiring nature of the site. The Elizabethan antiquary William Camden wrote that he had heard of "Hard Knott, an high steepe mountain, in the top whereof were discovered of late huge stones and foundations of a castle, not without great wonder, considering that it is so steepe and upright that one can hardly ascend up to it." His description leans more to the romantic than to the accurate, but it shows that the fort has long captured the imagination.

Eight hundred feet above sea level, the fort is nine miles from Ravenglass and eleven miles from Ambleside, not an equal day's march in each direction, the siting being with an eye to defence rather than to the lot of the toiling legionary. The views from it are superb when the weather is good. Frequently the weather is not good and it is interesting to consider what a young man from the Adriatic's Dalmatian coast thought of a posting here. It is difficult to imagine Hard Knott coming close to the top of any list of sought-after destinations. But the legionaries were provided with modern comforts. Between fort and road there are the ruins of a bath-house which had cold, warm and hot rooms and, nearby, a sauna. Here the men could relax, perhaps after having bashed the square of parade ground carved flat from the hillside to the side of the fort. Originally the fort itself would have been earth and timber. Later it was stone, with four gates, protecting an area of about two acres. Inside would have been a granary and barracks, with a stone-built house for the commander of the cohort of 500 troops.

Eventually Galava and Mediobogdum were evacuated, and legionaries no longer tramped the High Street. The Romans were recalled to the defence of the homeland in the early years of the fifth century and the country reverted to the control of the British, albeit the Romanised British. However here, as elsewhere in England and Wales, the Celtic tribal system gradually reasserted itself. This tribalism, which involved the setting up of minor kingdoms and the practice of dividing a king's land between his sons on his death, led to a sad lack of cohesion between the Celtic tribes, so that any invader found his job made simpler. To the south the invaders were Saxon, in the north they were Angles.

Soon after the departure of the Romans Lakeland formed a part of the kingdom of Rheged, whose most famous king was Urien, a name known to readers of Welsh folk history. Urien fought the Angles, besieging their holy island of Lindisfarne, but Rheged did not long survive his death, falling under the control of the kings of Strathclyde; and it was Strathclyde that the Angles fought as the new kingdom of Northumbria expanded westward. The Celts drew in upon themselves and, recognising their common ancestry, called themselves the Cymry, the fellow countrymen.

In the early part of the seventh century the Saxons defeated the "British" Celts at Dyrham, near Bristol, splitting the country in two and forcing the Celtic tribesmen into Cornwall and Cymru, that is Wales. And in the north the Angles were victorious at Chester, isolating the Welsh Cymry from those of Cumberland. The link between the Cumbrians, the Cornish, the Welsh and also the Celtic Britons of north-east France, can be seen in certain dialect words, there being no surviving Cumbrian language to prove the common origin. In the counting of sheep, for example, all the languages have *pimp* for five and *det* for ten, and similarities in the other numbers. There were local changes, however, and even within Lakeland there are quite marked differences. For eight, Coniston has *lowra*, while Borrowdale has *hovere* and Eskdale has *seckera*.

The Northumbrian expansion stopped short of Lakeland, the land at its edge being the most westerly of the Anglian lands: Westmaringaland, Westmoreland. Not surprisingly there are few Anglian sites in Lakeland, those that do exist being near the lowland border strip. Generally acknowledged as the best survival from the period is the seventh century inscribed cross of Bewcastle to the north-east of Carlisle. The Celts retreated before the Angles, up to the fells where they carried on as before, though with a much reduced homeland. There they stayed for 200 years until another invader arrived, one not bothered by the inclemency of the central Lakeland fells: the Norseman.

The Norseman of popular belief, the Viking, comes from Scandinavia, his long-boat disgorging a horde of horn-helmeted, pagan warriors hell-bent on rape, plunder and killing. It did happen like this, of course, but not always, and not here in Lakeland where the settlers arrived predominantly from Ireland and Man, probably refugees long settled in those islands but forced out by an invasion of the "real thing" from Norway. Ironically this invasion was prompted by a series of raids on Norway by the Vikings of Ireland!

The hardy Norse invaders did not stop at the lowland border of Lakeland. They were not perturbed by cold and wet and settled also in the uplands, and in doing so they left their mark indelibly on the land – not in the physical sense, although they cleared the forests, but in the naming of the place. They gave us fell from *fjall* – hill; dale from *dalr* – valley; beck from *bekkr* – stream; tarn from *tjorn* – small lake; gill from *gil* – gully; and force or foss from *foss* – waterfall. They gave us "thwaite", meaning a forest clearing, added to the end of many a place name. To prove their Irish connection they gave us *saeter*, Norse, and *erg*, Irish, meaning a summer pasture, as additions to place-names, chiefly as "-side" and "-er".

The new settlers, though several generations away from their Scandinavian homeland, were still Norse in their beliefs, holding to the Viking pantheon of gods. Pressure from the Christian Angles to the east – cultural rather than military pressure, although the borderlands were not always peaceful – caused a drift towards Christianity and the gradualness of this transition is beautifully illustrated on the magnificent sandstone cross at Gosforth. This cross, nearly fifteen feet high, dates from about 1000AD, and is inscribed on all four sides. The column is capped with a wheeled cross, but the lower shaft represents Yggdrasill, the sacred world ash tree, pure paganism. On the faces there are Heimdal, who guarded the bridge to Asgard; there is Odin; and there is a crucified Christ.

Elsewhere there is little, other than place-names, to see, though at Fell Foot in Little Langdale there is a raised terrace that is now widely believed to be a "thingmount" where "things" were held. These were courts, or assemblies, the instruments of government. The name survives to this day in Tynwald, the parliament of the Isle of Man.

Though it is relatively easy to trace the influence of settlers within Lakeland, the area was not sufficiently large or well-enough popu-lated to be a kingdom in its own right. Irrespective of which community of settlers held cultural sway over the uplands, Lakeland belonged to a larger kingdom. Even with Norse settlers installed, it was disputed by the new kingdom of England, and the old kingdom of Strathclyde. During the early part of the tenth century the English were dominant, but were gradually pushed southward. In 945 AD King Edmund returned with a Saxon army, and fought the British under the command of Domhnall. The battle went badly for the Saxons but eventually Domhnall was killed and the Cumbrians retired.

The Cumbrian warriors took the crown from the head of their dead king and threw it into a tarn. His body they buried under a large cairn of rocks. Each year warriors return, dredging the tarn with their spears until they find the crown, and carrying it to the cairn. There they knock to waken their king, calling on him to come again to lead them in the fight for their homeland. Each year he answers "Not yet, my warriors", and they return the crown to the tarn before disappearing into the misty uplands. The cairn is at Dunmail Raise, the high point of the A591 between Ambleside and Keswick. The tarn is Grisedale Tarn, to the east.

The cairn was moved when the road was widened; the battle may well have been fought at another site. King Edmund captured the two sons of Domhnall and had their eyes put out so they would represent no threat to him. One version of the story has Domhnall escaping to die in Rome. The intrusion of hard fact on legend is harsh, but it does not destroy the legend's power. The similarity of the story to that of the sleeping Arthur in Wales is the unmistakable mark of a people losing its homeland.

The English did not hold Cumbria, however, giving it to the Scottish King Malcolm I in an effort to secure a peaceful northern boundary. In 1032 it became part of England again when King Cnut exchanged it for Lothian in an arrangement at first sight strange, but, on reflection, perhaps no worse than the apparently arbitrary redistribution of villages and land between shires in the last county-boundary reorganisation.

In the wake of the Norman invasion of 1066 the Scots, now under Malcolm III, re-occupied Cumbria. The loss went unchallenged if not unnoticed by the Normans for twenty-five years, while they were engaged in the south – the area is not included in the Domesday survey because it lay in Scotland.

In 1092 William Rufus marched to Cumbria to view the northern border of his realm, and decided, as Hadrian had before him, that the Solway Firth was the obvious western end for a defenceable line, which meant that Cumbria must revert to the English crown. The area was occupied and a castle was built at Carlisle, but the ownership of the land was disputed over the next several centuries. Carlisle, not unnaturally in view of the castle, became the centre of attention. It was taken in 1135 by David of Scotland while England was disputed by Stephen and Matilda, and held until 1153 when Malcolm lost it to Henry II. William, the Lion, besieged the castle in 1174, but failed to win it, but Alexander II did re-occupy it in 1216, though only briefly. Henry III forced Alexander to retreat, and for five hundred years Cumbria remained English.

A characteristic of the Norman invasion of southern England was a surge of religious building. This was not confined to churches, but

included a large number of monasteries, the Norman lords being deeply religious and bestowing large tracts of land on the monastic orders. The first house founded in Cumbria was Carlisle Priory in 1123, the last Shap Abbey in 1199. Between the two there were half a dozen others including the most famous ones, Cartmell Priory and Furness Abbey. All except the last, Shap, were built on the low margin of Lakeland, and that nearness to the fells explains the density of the houses. For though anxious to prove their piety the Norman lords were not willing to offer the houses large pieces of valuable farmland from which taxes could easily be raised. Instead, smaller lowland areas were endowed, together with huge tracts of the upland wildernesses where population, and revenue, were sparse. All over Lakeland, as we shall see on our journey, the monastic houses held land.

This gift of high fell by the Norman lords was not, at first sight, over-generous, but it was to have far-reaching consequences, for the Lakeland houses were mainly Cistercian, and Cistercian houses from outside Cumbria also held large tracts – for example, Fountains Abbey owned Watendlath and Derwent Island. The Cistercians were a new order devoted to a life of austerity and hard work. This dedication to labour, together with the shrewd business sense of several excellent abbots, transformed Lakeland. Sheep were introduced to the fells, dairy herds to the dales. Farms were built, lakes fished and, at a later stage, there were the first stages of industrialisation with charcoal burning and metal working.

Such activities imply that peace had come to the area, but though Cumbria was never again, in any true sense, held by Scotland, it still saw skirmishes as the Scottish and English kings struggled for power at its border. Edward I, who had wanted Wales and so took it and encircled it with a stone ring of castles, also had designs on Scotland. He did not succeed in occupying the country, but did subdue it, defeating William Wallace. It was a short-lived success however, and the humiliation only fanned Scottish nationalism. The coming of Robert Bruce and the death of Edward overturned the balance of power in the border areas. Bruce invaded Cumbria in 1311, attacking the Lanercost Priory. The English retaliated and were roundly defeated at Bannockburn. The road to England was open, and the Scots took it in 1314. Carlisle was besieged in 1315, but not taken, and the low Lakeland border was attacked. Such attacks continued over the next six years, culminating in the "Great Raid" of 1322 when for three weeks the Scots devastated the area, plundering the abbey lands, looting farms and killing Cumbrians. In desperation the lord of Carlisle Castle, Sir Andrew de Harcla – who had been made Earl of Carlisle for his defence of the castle in 1315 – negotiated a settlement with the invaders. The Scots were bought off and returned north, appeased. Sir Andrew had restored peace to Cumbria, but his act was seen as treason, for which he was hanged and quartered.

The English kings offered Cumbria no security of their own, and for the next century its peace was shattered at intervals. Northern England was invaded again in 1345 and Carlisle was besieged three times between 1380 and 1387.

Not surprisingly the local lords were concerned for their safety. If they fought they would surely lose, if they negotiated they could hang as traitors. In many places a third option was exercised. The Scots when they came were a locust swarm, arriving, ravaging, departing, without any apparent desire to settle, or to lay siege – except to the obvious fortresses, such as Carlisle. A lord could therefore hope to survive an incursion if he could defend himself and his family for the few hours or days it took for the swarm to pass. To this end pele towers were built. These were square, with thick, strong walls of stone inside which a family could live on two or three floors. All over the low borders of Lakeland these towers exist – sometimes attached to a church – but they are rare in the fell country itself, because naturally the raids were made most often on the richer areas. However our journey will pass Kentmere Hall, a dale-built pele.

The fifteenth century finally brought a more peaceful time. Raids became fewer and less sustained, and by the turn of that century the area's economy was improving fast. The harmony on which this prosperity was based was, however, rudely shattered by Henry VIII's dissolution of the monasteries and the Northern revolt, "the Pilgrimage of Grace", that followed it. The Pilgrimage was put down hard and men from Cumbria died, in battle and in revenge.

In the rich farmland of the south of England, the monastic houses were landlords like any others, and the redistribution of their property had little direct effect on the livelihood of the peasant. In the north the houses used their wealth to alleviate the effects of poor soil and bad weather, and their loss must have been felt more keenly. As always, however, the departure of one regime instigated the arrival of another. The monasteries as clearing houses for manufactured articles and farm surplus were replaced by a circle of market towns – Cockermouth, Egremont, Kendal, Keswick. Twice more, though briefly, the peace of Lakeland was disturbed by advances from the north. In 1715 and 1745 the Scottish supporters of the Pretenders, Old and Young, came via Cumbria to further the Jacobite cause. In 1715 a local Cumbrian militia armed with agricultural implements turned out to stop the Scottish rebels on Penrith fell. They were led by Bishop Nicolson of Carlisle who heightened the unreal atmosphere by arriving at the battlefield in a coach. With the arrival of the Scots, chiefly the well-armed and notoriously ferocious Highlanders, the locals, wisely, melted away. The Jacobites moved southward, passing Kendal and Lancaster and finally frightening themselves into surrender at Preston. The adventure had taken less than four weeks.

In 1745 the Jacobite rising was in support of Bonny Prince Charlie and was a far more serious rebellion than that of 1715. The Scottish army reached Derby before retreating to the Highlands and eventual slaughter at Culloden. Again Cumbria escaped major disruption. Indeed the '45 was ultimately useful, in that the difficulties of marching an army through the area led to improvements in the road system.

Within twenty-five years of the last of the executions in the wake of the '45. William Gilpin had arrived in Lakeland, in search of the picturesque, and one William Wordsworth was born in Cockermouth.

INDUSTRIAL HISTORY

Today's Lakeland hardly conjures up a picture of a highly industrialised area and so it is surprising to find the extent to which the growth of industry has influenced the modern landscape. While the outlying parts of the district provided, and still provide, good agricultural land, the uplands sustain, on average, only about one sheep per acre. In contrast, the central area is rich in mineral deposits, first mentioned by Agricola.

There is copper in the Coniston area, iron in Borrowdale and other minerals including small amounts of gold and silver, though there is no tin. In the lowland areas there is, in addition, coal beneath the coastal plain to the west.

A major collection of swords and spears discovered close to the Roman fort at Ambleside in 1741 was at first believed, not unnaturally, to be Roman. It is now known that the weapons pre-date the Roman invasion by many centuries, and some of the detailed markings on them resemble those found in other parts of Cumbria, suggesting an early industry. But even this is not the first suggestion of industrial development in Lakeland. That was probably located on the steep slopes of Pike of Stickle, one of Langdale Pikes. In the upper reaches of Stickle Beck many rough Stone Age tools have been discovered and it is now believed that the area was a major source of such implements. The original site, identified in 1921 and thought to have Neolithic connections, was no more than some ten feet square. About a dozen other sites have since been identified, over a far wider area, including some on the slopes of Glaramara and Scafell Pike. Radio-carbon dating of sample tools found on the Langdale sites have given a date around 2300BC. Possibly the men who worked on these various sites co-ordinated their activities. We cannot be sure – but we do know that Lakeland tools were distributed quite widely.

The Romans certainly mined lead and used local slates on their buildings, but it was when development came under the stewardship of the Cistercian Abbots of Furness Abbey, whose lands covered most of the region, that industrialisation began in earnest. The western part of their possessions was largely forest which the monks used to produce charcoal, the main fuel of the time. Charcoal was used to smelt iron from the red haematite ores which had also been discovered locally. The charcoal burning process was, however, demanding of timber, since it requires five tons of wood to produce one ton of charcoal, and three tons of charcoal were needed to produce one ton of iron. The forests were therefore a good deal depleted by the time of the Abbey's dissolution in 1537.

As well as its importance to the fledgling iron industry, charcoal was also used in tanning and in the manufacture of gunpowder, the latter located at several sites, principally around Kendal and Elterwater. The Commissioners' report at the dissolution of Furness Abbey includes a section on the Abbey's woodland resources – "There ys moche wood growing in Furneysfells in the mounteynes there . . ." This wood was used in "a Smythey and sometyme two or three kepte for making of Yron . . ." and for "makyng of Coles". The woodland was "to the yerely valewe by estymacion of xiijli. vjs, vijd"!

"The making of Coles" is charcoal burning, carried out by burners who until the early part of this century lived in wigwam-shaped huts in the Furness forests. Both huts and burners are well described in Arthur Ransome's *Swallows and Amazons*. Charcoal is made by the controlled burning of wood with limited air supply. Oak, birch, hazel and alder trees were coppiced to ensure a good supply of coppice poles for making the basic stack of fuel. This was earth-covered to exclude air and the poles were fired. About twenty-four hours later the whole was dowsed and the charcoal raked out. Juniper wood was used in stacks on its own as it was used specifically in the making of gunpowder and was highly prized.

The charcoal burners were known as colliers, a term taken over by the coal-mining industry when coal replaced wood as primary fuel. Lakeland's coal lies near Whitehaven. The reserves were difficult to work, but substantial, amounting to some 310 million tons beneath the coastal plain with an estimated further 260 million tons beneath the sea within five miles of the coast. By 1815 the Whitehaven mines produced some 450,000 tons a year, the largest of the mines being owned by Sir John Lowther, employer of William Wordsworth's father.

The Lowther family, in effect, ran Cumbria for centuries, Sir James Lowther being created first Earl of Lonsdale in 1794. It was he who largely promoted the local industrial revolution, and even today, the family is by far the largest private landowner in the area, holding over 45,000 acres.

Coal production reaching a peak of 2.3 million tonnes in 1909. It remained at around this rate for about fifteen years, but thereafter declined. By 1958 production was down to one million tons per year, a rate suggested in 1974 for opencast mining from the North Lakeland area. This projected rate, though appearing to be on the high side, is causing considerable concern over its potential environmental effects.

Our ancestors were too preoccupied with earning a living to be concerned, like us, about the environment, a point amply testified to by innumerable disused mine workings and quarries around Lakeland. And strangely, far from defacing the landscape, in many cases these add to its character.

The first mining company, properly speaking, to be set up in the Lakeland area was that running the Goldscope and Dale Head mines. Goldscope, at the head of the Newlands Valley and named from a corruption of God's Hope, has a history that can be traced back to the time of Henry III, and during its early years within the newly-formed company it was largely worked by a group of specially imported German miners. The mine supplied iron ore to a smelting plant in Keswick that was the largest in England at the time. During the eighteenth century the mine closed for financial reasons, though it later re-opened under new ownership. The industrial revolution was by then in full swing, but the cost of modernising the mine forced three of the four owners to pull out of the enterprise. The lone survivor, A. Clarke, was – in the best tradition of such stories – later rewarded with the large profits which had for so long eluded the mine's owners. (He did far better than Thomas Pierce, the Earl of Westmorland, two centuries earlier. Elizabeth I had then claimed the mine on the grounds that it contained gold and silver, and Earl was executed for treason because he had the temerity to contest the case.)

As the smelting industry developed in central Lakeland, there were furnaces in Great Langdale, supplied by two mines at the foot of Fairfield, and another in the Langstrath Valley which was fed via Ore Gap, between Esk Pike and Bow Fell. Further down Eskdale, rich veins of haematite had been found and a number of mines were developed. The trade became so important that a railway opened to carry ore from the mines to the coast at Ravenglass, and on to the new iron and steel mills of South Wales. This railway was never a success as a freightline and, after being rebuilt as a narrow gauge railway, now earns its living carrying enthusiastic tourists.

With plentiful supplies of good ore, it is hardly surprising that the iron trade flourished. Henry Bessemer developed his process locally, and larger scale operations led to the merging of the various companies to form the United Steel Company in 1919. At that time the production of ore, mainly in the far west of the region, reached 1.25 million tons annually, in those days worth some £900,000. Nowdays the local mines are no longer economic, and the remaining iron works use imported ores.

Copper mining dwindled faster than iron mining, and was over by the end of the nineteenth century due to reduced demand coupled with overseas competition. In 1855 ore production had been some 300 tons per month, employing about 500 miners, whose average pay was just under £1 a week. At first the ore-bearing rocks used to be split by being dowsed with water after first being heated. Later, gunpowder was used, but was a hazardous business, particularly before the advent of the safety fuse in 1870 (prior to that the powder was ignited by straws, which the miners themselves had to provide). The ore from the Coniston mines was carried over the fells to smelters at Keswick which had become the hub of Lakeland's industry.

By the early nineteenth century in addition to smelting, a pencil industry was well established in Keswick, using graphite found in upper Borrowdale. The graphite was found as plumbago, better known locally as wadd, black-cawke or black lead. The date of its discovery is a mystery, but appears to have been sometime in the early part of the sixteenth century. It is thought to have been used initially in lumps, as a crayon to mark sheep: one story ascribes the first use to the monks of Furness Abbey. Following continental trends, the crayons developed into pencils. In earlier times, however, the main uses of graphite were "the casting of bomb-shells, round shot and cannon-balls". And all from the tranquility of Borrowdale!

Other uses for wadd included the glazing of pottery, dyeing, and medicinal uses. It was reputedly a cure for the colic, the dosage being as much as would lie on a sixpenny piece, taken in white wine or ale. The wadd mines were largely exhausted by 1840, although stocks did keep the pencil manufacturers going for a while. After 1906 no

41

genuine Borrowdale plumbago remained. A large pencil factory remains active in Keswick today, but it uses imported graphite.

Not far away from the old wadd workings at Seathwaite, quarrying continues at the head of Honister pass, though here it is for green slate, perhaps the most characteristic of all the materials to come from Lakeland. The Honister quarries are believed to date back to 1643 and were certainly in full operation a hundred years later. Slates were carried from the quarries by pack horse, along Moses sled-gate, via the side of Great Gable to Wasdale Head and then to the coast. Other slate quarries around the Coniston Fells had a significant advantage in this respect: slates were loaded on to boats and shipped the length of Windermere for subsequent export by sea. By 1805 the production of slate from the Coniston Fells exceeded 25,000 tons a year. Their advantage over the Honister quarries was further enhanced with the introduction of a railway to the lakeside at Coniston in 1859, while the remote Honister quarries were communicating with their office in Keswick by carrier pigeon. Slate extraction today is only about ten per cent of the levels in the last century; but, against all odds, the Buttermere Green Slate Company is still operating the Honister Quarries.

Probably the oldest metal extraction industry in Lakeland was lead mining, which did not end until the long-established and very profitable Greenside mine closed in 1962. Its near neighbour, the Helvellyn mine, had been more characteristic of the region's lead mining in having a chequered history and shareholders who often became restless over poor results. Eventually, in 1880, the Helvellyn mine's site was bought by the Manchester Corporation Water Works.

In 1868 the MCWW had engaged the services of the famous water supply engineer, J.F. Bateman, to advise them on how to meet the demands of their rapidly growing city and its expanding textile industry. Bateman proposed that water should be taken from Ullswater or Haweswater, but in due course it was Thirlmere that was chosen: the water level was to be raised by 54 feet, which would increase the lake's surface area from 330 acres to 812 acres. This clash between the needs of development and of conservation, of a kind which has become so familiar, naturally aroused a great deal of local hostility.

It was not, however, the first reservoir to be proposed in Lakeland.

Thirlmere

One had been built thirty years earlier at the head of Kentmere, to provide power for the industries of Kendal which included mills for bobbins, wool, paper and corn, finishing mills for marble and iron, and a gunpowder factory. Bateman had been behind that dam, too, employed by a consortium of mill-owners. His first grand scheme for five reservoirs had eventually shrunk to one, largely because of the cost involved.

Purchase of 48 acres of land	£960
Building of dam	£6150
Building of keeper's cottage	£15

– that was the estimate tendered by the Manchester firm of Shuttle-worth and Dobson for Kentmere, and it had shocked the consortium – although they accepted it – by exceeding Bateman's forecast by sixty per cent. And then the actual cost of the dam turned out to be exactly twice as much! Clearly over-optimistic estimates are not a modern phenomenon.

Kentmere ceased to be a working reservoir during the 1930s, although the commissioners, set up by the enabling act signed by Queen Victoria in 1845, are still responsible for the safety of the dam.

The chief difference between the Kentmere and Thirlmere projects was that the latter would supply water to a community outside Lakeland. Bateman had little time for what he described as "a sentimental idea that it was sacrilege to invade the precincts of the Lakes for any such utilitarian purposes as giving a supply of water to famishing thousands of the manufacturing district." But it is understandable that Lakelanders resented the submerging of acres of their land for other people's benefit – the start of an inevitable process by which their countryside would be more influenced by distant industrial development than by their own activities. The demands for water and timber over the past century have had a major effect on the appearance of several Lakeland valleys.

Bateman died a year before the first stone of the Thirlmere dam was laid in 1890. The MCWW decided that it must control the lake's entire catchment area of 11,000 acres, and the acquisition of these lands led to many legal battles – one result of which was the strengthening of the concept of compulsory purchase, used all too often in later years.

There are now two lakes reserved exclusively for the supply of water: Thirlmere and Haweswater, both schemes of the MCWW and administered today by its descendant, the North West Water Authority. About 140 million gallons a day are taken from the two lakes together, which may seem a small amount given their capacity, but is enough, with evaporation, to lower their levels very significantly during dry summers so that the village of Mardale, drowned under Haweswater, presents its outline to the world once more.

During the exceptionally dry summer of 1984 Mardale was exposed for several months, and the valley drew crowds of visitors after being reported on television news in July. By then its upper end had been dry for some time, and not only had grass and other vegetation begun to grow on the floor of the lake, but this growth was already being put to good grazing use by sheep. It seems unlikely that seeds submerged for so long can have remained viable, so perhaps the wind, and birds, explain this rapid renewal of growth. It was a striking illustration of the temporary nature of man's handiwork.

After obtaining an Act of Parliament for Haweswater in 1919,

Mardale revealed, 1984

Manchester Corportation made no move for the next ten years. The dam was constructed to its present height in 1934. In the face of fierce opposition to its scheme, Manchester very nearly accepted a compromise proposal which called for a lower water level, but a drought in the summer of 1934 convinced the authorities of the need for the full reservoir capacity. It is ironic that very dry summers which from time to time bring Mardale into view are precisely the conditions which led to its death.

In the 1970's MCWW put forward a new scheme to raise the level of Haweswater by a further 115 feet. The proposal has not yet proceeded far, but has not completely died. Raising the waterline to this extent would clearly have a dramatic effect on what is left of the valley. Watch this space – literally.

Whilst the industrial areas of south Lancashire were gaining water from the eastern side of Lakeland, Whitehaven began to obtain its water from Ennerdale Water in 1947 and the level of the lake was raised by 4^1/$_2$ feet in 1962. However this was hardly significant and the Ennerdale valley is dominated by another man-made feature: its forest.

Some 5000 years ago much of Lakeland was natural forest, but with the development of agriculture and the demand for charcoal the forests receded. The first large-scale planting in the area took place in the early years of the twentieth century, by none other than our old friend MCWW. About 1,950 acres of plantations were established around the Thirlmere reservoir to help consolidate the catchment slopes and to enhance rainfall(!).

In 1919 the Government set up the Forestry Commission: one body, but now with divided objectives. Initially it was intended to build up wood supplies, and to aid rural employment and local economies. More recently, however, greater emphasis has been laid on conservation.

The Commission owns about ten per cent of Lakeland, the largest forests being Ennerdale, Grizedale and Thornthwaite. Planting began at Ennerdale in 1926, and ten years later a White Paper was issued outlining plans for vast afforestation of Eskdale, Dunnerdale and Ennerdale.

When the scheme did go ahead, there were gains for the conservationists too, for in 1936 an agreement was reached with the Commission that the central area of the district, containing the high fells, would not be planted.

Today the Lakeland forests employ about 400 people and have an annual production of some 80,000 cubic metres of timber. If we consider typical planks, 12ft by 9 inches by 2 inches, this figure would correspond to about 2 million of them – but of course, not all the production takes this form. From Grizedale, for instance, twenty per cent of the timber goes to saw milling, forty-five per cent to the manufacture of paper and board, while posts and stakes account for the remainder. Very little of this wood is now processed within the district.

The Grizedale forest, like much of Lakeland, was administered by the Cistercian monks of Furness Abbey during the Middle Ages. Following the dissolution of the monasteries, there was a falling off in forestry activity, but by the mid-eighteenth century trees, mainly larch, were being planted by the Ainslies of Grizedale Hall to provide

props for the iron ore mines. So the Forestry Commission perpetu-
ates a long tradition and, given its current attitude towards conservation, its woods ought not to be too offensive to lovers of Lakeland.

THE WALKS

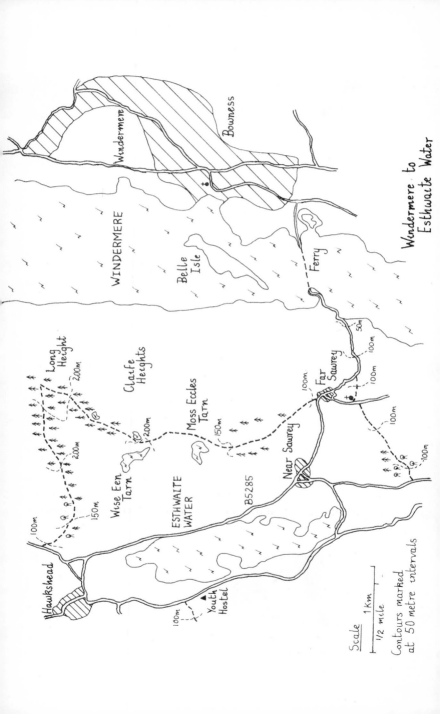

Windermere to Esthwaite Water

Hawkshead

WINDERMERE

Windermere

Bowness

Belle Isle

Ferry

Long Height

200m

Clawfe Heights

200m

Moss Eccles Tarn

150m

Wise Een Tarn

200m

200m

150m

100m

Far Sawrey

100m

50m

100m

100m

100m

Near Sawrey

ESTHWAITE WATER

B5285

Youth Hostel

100m

Scale

1 Km

1/2 mile

Contours marked at 50 metre intervals

WINDERMERE TO ESTHWAITE WATER

The visitor with little architectural knowledge, standing in the main streets of Windermere village on a cold winter's day, would be surprised to learn that the village is less than 150 years old. If he came again in midsummer, to be jostled by the crowds eager to reach the sourvenir shops, he would better understand why the town exists at all.

It is here because the railway finishes here. It mattered little in 1845, when it was decided to push the track lakewards from Kendal, that the proposed terminal village was a good step away from the target, England's largest lake. What was needed was the name; so the little village of Birthwaite was submerged, figuratively at least, by Windermere. Today the older name survives as the name of the road leading off towards the water from the main road, near the library. This road passes Queen Adelaide's Hill, which was named to commemorate a trip by the Queen in July 1840 – before that it was called Green Hill. This name change, too, was in the interests of popularity. The Queen's visit had encouraged visitors, who brought wealth. The local enthusiasm for the tourist industry has even extended to the construction of a fine memorial to M.J.B. Baddeley in thanks for his guide to Lakeland published in 1886.

William Wordsworth wrote a sonnet against the extension of the railway beyond Kendal, and was barely placated by the decision not to carry it on, as was first planned, beyond Windermere (or rather the then Birthwaite) to the lake itself, and towards Grasmere. Wordsworth feared the encroachment of modernity on the Lakeland scene – a fear that can be understood by those concerned with today's environment. In 1899 a cheap round-trip system was in operation, with a combined ticket for railway and Windermere steamer. The system was "slowly, but surely, ruining, sentimentally, the Windermere district".

It is too easy to be critical of many of today's visitors who seek to impose their requirements for entertainment on the area. Let us, instead concentrate on the positive. Windermere village has much that is worthy of note. Rayrigg Hall, at the end of Birthwaite Road, is a fine manorial house of the early eighteenth century that was, for a short time around the late 1780's, the home of William Wilberforce. A mile of so north is Calgarth Hall, a similar house. But there is a difference, this Hall being the scene of one of the most famous Lakeland hauntings. Myles Phillipson, an early owner of the Hall and its surrounding parkland, coveted the land owned by a respectable old couple, Kraster and Dorothy Cook. No amount of legal persuasion could remove the couple so Phillipson gave them a pie baked to include his family's silver spoons. The squire then sent the constable to the Cook's cottage, and he arrested the couple for theft. Though loudly protesting their innocence, and Phillipson's injustice, the Cooks were tried, convicted and sentenced to death. After the sentence was passed Dorothy cursed Phillipson, saying that the couple would haunt him until every inch of his land was taken from him.

There must have been considerable local support for the old couple, but even so they were executed. Phillipson had little time to enjoy his triumph, for immediately after the execution two grinning skulls appeared in a wall niche of Calgarth Hall. Unnerved by the experience – and who would not be – Phillipson threw the skulls into the centre of the lake in his park.

Two versions of the haunting now exist. In one the hall was filled with shrieking that could only be silenced by dredging the lake until the skulls were recovered and replaced in the niche where their hideous grinning wore the squire down. In that version Phillipson also tried burying the skulls with the same result. In the other version the skulls simply re-appeared in the wall niche. In this version Phillipson tries again to rid himself of the bones, having them first buried, then burnt and finally crushed to powder and scattered; but all to no avail, the skulls return to their niche each time. Eventually Phillipson was left a broken man without land or money, though how he lost them is not satisfactorily explained. Did he spend his all in trying to rid himself of the curse? Or was he driven to drinking it all away?

The house passed to Dr Watson, Bishop of Llandaff, but (curiously, in view of Dorothy Cook's quite specific curse) the haunting appears to have gone on. Eventually Dr Watson, lacking the services of Sherlock Holmes that his more famous name-sake could have called on, exorcised the spirit of the skulls and, for good measure, walled them up. Behind their wall, they grin still. Or so it is said.

In passing it can be noted that Dr Watson was an interesting cleric. Though Bishop of Llandaff for over thirty years he appears never to have visited Cardiff, his only contact with his see being the drawing of his salary. He spent his time at Calgarth making plans to increase his estate by draining a hundred acres of lake, and planting trees. He was a prodigious planter and incurred the wrath of William Wordsworth when he, along with John Curwen of Belle Isle, made extensive use of the imported larch. (The Forestry Commission's regiments of conifers have few admirers, today, but the larch is still a fine tree, whatever Wordsworth thought.)

The best view of the tree-lined shores of this middle section of Windermere is obtained from Orrest Head, reached from a path opposite the railway station. The hillock derives its name from *orrosta*, a Norse word for battle, suggesting that some ancient but long-forgotten skirmish took place here. It is sad to think that at this spot, with its magnificent view, men fought and died for something so important that no one can remember it.

Our route does not visit Orrest Head, unless the traveller cares to start there, but makes for Bowness-on-Windermere, and the lake. Today the villages of Windermere and Bowness merge along the main road, but Bowness was once separate. It is also an older settlement, though most of what we now see dates from the mid-nineteenth century. The church gives the true age away, having been consecrated in 1483 and dedicated to St Martin. Outside it is a fine building, well set, but inside it shows the handiwork of Victorian "restorers". One survival from an earlier age, from 1629, is a Latin inscription commemorating the failure of the Gunpowder Plot. It is the work of Christopher Phillipson, whose family held Belle Isle for the Royalists in the Civil War. The chancel is built over a plot of land once known as the eight-and-forty row, which holds the victims of the worst ever accident on the lake. The register of Grasmere church records the names of forty-six dead and states that there were also two or three others, and seven horses – and on "the XXth of Octob: 1635 theis were all drowned in Windermer Water in one boate cameinge over from Hawkshead". Another version has forty-seven people and eleven horses dead – as usual the witnesses were unreliable. It is thought that the victims were a wedding party caught in a storm that produced very bad flooding in the district. Of the actual accident a contemporary account notes: "Launch'd had they scarcely to the middle of the water, being scarcely a mile broad, but the Boat, either through some pressure of weight which discharged her, or some violent and imperious windes and waves which surprised her, with all her people, became drench'd in the depths". At that time the ferry would have been only a rowed boat, and it is believable that nearly fifty people, together with perhaps a dozen horses, would have made it unstable.

Leaving St Martin's, the traveller heading lakeward also leaves Bowness, his route finding and hugging the shore-line around Cockshott Point towards the Nab, and the modern ferry. The shore-line here epitomises the conflict within the Lake District National Park between entertainment, recreation and conservation. The traveller can be surprised by Sealink ships – very surprised if he thought they were confined to ferrying cars to France; can see enough expensive water transport to make an Arab sheikh envious; can buy an ice-cream and can feed innumerable ducks and gulls to a backdrop of wooded lakeside and distant hills.

Windermere is the largest of all English lakes, over ten miles long, though never wider than a mile; a ribbon of a lake filling the hollow formed an age ago when ice was spilling down from Langdale. The name is said to derive from *Vinand*, a Norse name, presumably a chieftain, who owned this *mere*, or lake. Because of the structure of the Norse language the water would be the "lake of Vinand", with "of Vinand" being written *Vinandar*, but coming before *mere*. Thus *Vinandarmere*. Usage, or rather misusage, has shortened the name to the now common form, but many old books and texts retain the longer spelling. Camden, the Elizabethan traveller and writer, thought the area was worthy of note "for among these mountains the greatest standing water in all England now called Winandermere lieth stretched out."

Because of its sheer size Windermere virtually defies a description based on anything except an accumulation of facts. It is, locally, divided into three "cubbles", the Bowness ferry crossing the middle one. This cubble, and the northern one towards Ambleside, are the tourist water. The southern cubble, extending almost to Newby Bridge, is quieter and more remote. But along the length these generalisations fail.

Windermere has over a dozen islands, all "holmes" in best old Norse tradition, most of which are mere specks of earth on the vast

Windermere, looking south

acreage of water. According to Camden, hermits inhabited each of Windermere's islands. At Derwent Water we shall read of more, and more famous, hermits on islands. It seems that there have been times in English history when so many wanted to enjoy (endure?) the solitary life afforded by islands that hermits stood shoulder to shoulder.

The largest island is the appropriately named Long Holme, the name of which was changed to Belle Isle when the Island was bought by Isabella Curwen in 1781. It is the only island now inhabited, and has been inhabited for a long time (there is evidence of Roman islanders), its isolation and almost complete security having always been obvious. The island was held for the Royalist cause during the Civil War. By the early seventeenth century, however, warfare had moved on from the hit-and-move-on tactics that made fortresses so important. Belle Isle may have been an insult to Cromwell's Puritan sense of order and, perhaps, a minor irritation to local Roundheads, but it was hardly worth a water-borne invasion. The leader of the Royalists, Robin Phillipson – Robin the Devil – was clearly aggravated by being ignored, and hearing that Colonel Briggs, the local Cromwellian leader, was in church at Kendal, he set out in pursuit. Reaching the church, The Devil rode in through the main door with murder in mind to discover that he had been misinformed – Briggs was not there. What was present was a Cumbrian congregation, less than thrilled by the sacrilege, who turned on him and blocked his way back to the door. Phillipson therefore spurred his horse through a little low side entrance, losing his helmet, and almost his head. The helmet, the Rebel's Cap, is still in the church.

Visitors to the Isle can walk among the gardens and visit the Round House, not named for an eventual Roundhead victory, but for its shape.

South of Belle Isle spits of land on both the eastern and western shores reduce Windermere's width to about 600 yards. At this point there has been a ferry certainly for 500 years and probably for longer. The earliest reference is in 1454 when "Henry Belyngham, farmer of the fishery of said water, claims to have the said passage". Belyngham paid ten shillings for the privilege of running the service, a rent that had risen to £6 a century later. What Belyngham charged is not recorded, though the price for a man or horse was 2d in 1884. The ferry rights were prized, and if you stand car-less at Bowness and contemplate the lake barrier between you and Hawkshead, it is easy to see why. In 1870 the row-boat ferry service was finally replaced by a wire rope which, when it snapped one day, left the ferry rudderless and helplessly drifting. After that incident a guide rope was added to the system. The ferry of those days, loaded up with a coach and four, must have been an impressive sight. Today an efficient, though unromantic, boat plies the lake.

Our route uses the ferry to cross Windermere, but choose a clear day. In the days of the rowed ferry the locals lived in awe of the mist-hidden Crier of Claife who lured passengers and boatmen alike to their deaths by the power of his voice. Only one ferryman who responsed to a cry of "Boat!" through the mist came back alive. His face was a mask of horror and before he recovered from his speechless terror he died. So just what it is that dwells among John Curwen's alien larch trees we still do not know.

Windermere at Bowness

From the centre of the lake the view northward is blocked by Belle Isle, but the southern half of Windermere can be seen disappearing down towards Newby Bridge. It is then that some idea can be gained of the length of the lake. Not surprisingly this expanse of water has attracted attention. On 2nd September 1911 Joseph D. Foster, the

Oldham swimming champion, made the first recorded swim along its length. At the time this was a remarkable feat – today it has become an annual race. In 1930 Sir Henry Seagrave set a world water speed record on the lake when *Miss England* II achieved 98.8 mph. On his next attempt Sir Henry and his engineer Victor Halliwell were killed. The lure of speed on the big lakes has had a similar effect on boatmen to the Crier of Claife.

One feature of the lake that surprises the visitor, particularly if he comes only in summer time when the sun bouncing off the flat surface dazzles the eyes, is that the lake has frequently been frozen solid. The most recent freezing was in the winter of 1962/63 and it seems that earlier centuries were colder more often. In 1895 the ice was solid from shore to shore for over six weeks, and a hundred years earlier there was wrestling as well as skating on the ice, and an ox was roasted. It can be said that the lake came of age in 1928, however. In that year someone drove a car on it.

At the centre of the lake the water below the ferry is over 200 feet deep. Windermere is second only to Wast Water in depth, and some idea of the effect of glaciation can be gained from the fact that the lake bed is 80 foot below mean sea level. There is a lot of water in Windermere, about 90 thousand million gallons. Not surprisingly there are also a lot of fish. Chiefly these are perch, trout and char, and the vast potential harvest has attracted interest from the Middle Ages. In earlier times the three cubbles were rented out and sometimes sub-let for the netting of fish. In 1921 commercial fishing ended, after having been continuous for over seven hundred years. However, during World War II the vast quantities of small perch attracted the interest of a hungry nation. The fish were caught, canned and sold as perchines! In the first year twenty-five tons of fish were landed, but the trade did not survive the coming of peace.

Despite its fish population Windermere is hardly a bird-watcher's paradise. There are few breeding ducks, though there is a good population of red-breasted mergansers, and many divers and grebes over-winter. The chief delight is that the lake's length, and its north-south orientation, means that it is on many migration paths and fine collections of birds can be seen stopping over near the water.

On the far side of the ferry our route follows the road westward, a road that is thoughtfully provided with signs for queuing drivers at 15, 30 and 45 minute waits. The road passes a cove with a fine

collection of boats, sedges and swans that swim towards the approaching walker, having learned that tourist means sandwich.

The road goes uphill and bears right, signposted Hawkshead. Just beyond Hawkrigg farm, at (382 952), a signed footpath leads off west to St Peter's church, the parish church of Far Sawrey, which is a considerable distance from the hamlet. The church can be seen across the fields, simple and with an upright dignity.

From the church go left and after a short distance another signed footpath leads off right, south-westward, at (377 951). At lambing time, in very early spring, this signpost carries (as do all others in the National Park) a notice requesting walkers to exercise caution when crossing the land. It must be remembered that though the path follows a right of way, it does so across someone's land. Please do not assume that a right of way bestows rights of all kinds. Access onto open spaces in England is a delicate matter and could be prejudiced by bad-mannered behaviour on farmland. As a walker you will be received in the light of the antics of the walker who preceded you. Be aware that the man behind you will be judged on your behaviour.

The pathway at (377 951) is followed – note that the path actually goes off in well-defined style but at right angles to the sign pointer. The walker soon touches real south lakeland, beautiful trees growing on bracken-covered, boulder-strewn slopes. The path is at all times well-defined through the final woodland section to the lane at (369 944). Go right, north, along the lane to a junction at (368 954). Left from here is Esthwaite Water, right is Near Sawrey and Hill Top Farm.

To Return

The best return route is to continue around the western side of Esthwaite Water to Hawkshead, the village famous for being where Wordsworth went to school.

From Hawkshead take the B5285 for Sawrey and go left at (355 981) and left again at (358 983). Take the path right (east) at (359 986) and follow it up Long Height. At (377 987) take the path southward which is followed past beautiful tarn scenery to the road at Far Sawrey. Go left to return to the ferry.

Distances

From Windermere church to Esthwaite Water $-7^{1}/_{2}$km
Return route via Hawkshead -12km

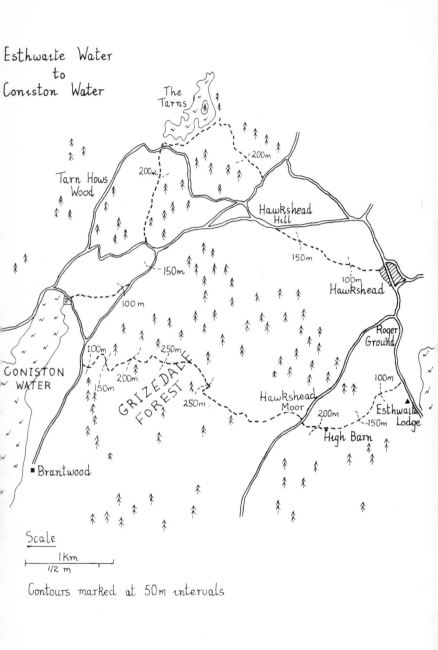

Esthwaite Water to Coniston Water

The Tarns

Tarn Hows Wood

200m

200m

Hawkshead Hill

150m

150m

100m

Hawkshead

100m

Roger Ground

150m

CONISTON WATER

100m

250m

GRIZEDALE FOREST

200m

150m

250m

Hawkshead Moor

200m

100m

Esthwaite Lodge

150m

High Barn

Brantwood

Scale

1 Km

1/2 m

Contours marked at 50m intervals

ESTHWAITE WATER TO CONISTON WATER

If William Wordsworth is the man of Lakeland, then Beatrix Potter is the woman. Hill Top, where she lived after her marriage, receives more visitors in a year than either Dove Cottage or Rydal Mount – though not than the two combined. It is only a few hundred yards north of our route, at Sawrey, and is worth the detour. Beatrix Potter's beautiful little books for children still exercise a fascination over eighty years after the publication of *The Tale of Peter Rabbit*.

Helen Beatrix Potter was born on July 28, 1866, and by the standards of our day she had a deprived childhood. There were few playthings, few walks, little contact with children of her own age apart from her brother Bertram, and not much more even with adults, except her nanny. Her diet was a succession of lamb lunches and rice puddings. Her father, a qualified barrister but of independent means who spent the day in his club, was a gifted amateur photographer who appears not to have taken much interest in his children, although he did produce an excellent photographic record of Beatrix's formative years.

When her brother went to school Beatrix was even more isolated and lonely, developing, as such children often do, a secret handwriting for her diaries. She also began to draw, and from an early age exhibited a considerable talent. Cocooned in her third floor room in London, there would have been few subjects for her talents, but occasional family holidays – to the country, Scotland and Lakeland – introduced her to ferns and animals, and she drew on this experience for her sketches. Her love for animals, and a need for subjects, led her to keep pets. One was significant: a hedgehog called Tiggy.

Her interest in plants went beyond using them simply as subjects for drawing. She was a serious botanist. She missed out on being the first to propose, but proposed independently of the German scholar who *was* the first, that lichens were symbiotic. She had a paper on spore production published by the London Linnaean Society and was offered work by the Natural History Museum. And she also drew mouse-holes and rabbit's grocery shops.

During one family holiday, taken at Wray Castle, Beatrix showed her sketches and writings to Canon Rawnsley, a famous Lakeland name, then vicar of Wray. He was enchanted, persuading her that they should be published. In 1901, when she was thirty-five, she published *The Tale of Peter Rabbit* privately. It sold 250 copies and made about £12. In 1902 Frederick Warne also published it. In the years to 1913 twenty further books were published. After 1913 her writing virtually ceased. A couple of works were published, written, apparently, for the American market and neither exceptionally good nor very successful. She had, however, continued her coded diaries right into middle age, and the discovery of these, in 1952, and their deciphering and publication, allows some insight into her character. She was possessed of a sharp and agile mind, and collected fascinating information rather in the way a jackdaw collects shiny objects. She reports the death in Paris of a woman aged 107 who had witnessed the execution of Louis XVI. She notes that nannies in Berlin need licences for prams and even then are confined to their own streets.

Beatrix was engaged in 1905 to Frederick Warne's son, Norman; an engagement of which her parents disapproved partly for snobbish reasons – Norman was a tradesman – and partly because it did not fit with their idea of Beatrix's role as dutiful and obedient daughter. Norman died of leukaemia shortly after the engagement. But Beatrix did marry, becoming Mrs William Heelis on 14 October 1913, when she was forty-seven years old. Heelis was a Lakeland solicitor whom Beatrix had met when she bought Castle Farm, the property next to Hill Top, in 1905, and again her parents felt he was beneath her. But this time Beatrix held to her purpose. Despite having owned Hill Top for eight years she had never lived permanently in Lakeland, being still part of the furniture in her parent's Kensington home. On marrying William she moved to Lakeland for good, living at Castle Farm for the last thirty years of her life.

The change between Miss Beatrix Potter and Mrs William Heelis was extraordinary. Warnes were instructed not to divulge her new name or address, and anyone who did find her and asked for a few words got just that. And very blunt words, too, by all accounts.

As a child Beatrix had been very shy, probably as a result of her isolation, and she does appear in later life to have been brusque, even impolite. Perhaps her natural awkwardness with people as a result of not having to deal with them when young, coupled with her desire for acceptance as a person rather than as the creator of Mrs Tiggy

Winkle, made her slightly insensitive. Certainly she made few local friends, no one being too keen to face her rudeness and withering stare.

She farmed Hill Top and Castle Farm with the help of managers, breeding Herdwick sheep. It is now customary to tell of her skill with the sheep and how in later life she became an expert on them, but the reality seems to be that she farmed as a hobby, and that although she did know a lot about the sheep, she could make mistakes. Her last farm manager was sceptical of her true worth as a farmer, claiming that she could not know anything, coming as she did from London. That is prejudice, but conceals grains of truth. Everyone was pleased that she did not live up to her wealth and fame however. She dressed in farm-hand style, old coats and a sack around the shoulders. So scruffy did she become that once a tramp who met her in a lane greeted her as one of his own kind, which delighted her.

On 22 December, 1943, with William at her side and the Lakeland hills before her, she died. Her ashes were scattered at a secret spot, known only to her last farm manager.

The reaction of people who know nothing of Beatrix Potter's work, when they are given a copy of one of her books, varies from enchantment to perplexity as to why there is such a fuss. The books have spawned a considerable industry – there is even a Tailor's House in Gloucester selling books and mementoes. But it is notice-able that many visitors to Hill Top are adults. Today's children, more worldly with their exposure to Star Wars and the Incredible Hulk, are less impressed. But the books have stood the test of time. They have been translated into many languages – the visitor to France will recognise the characters in *Pierre Lapin*. Beatrix Potter is an institu-tion and, as such, will run and run.

And Sawrey church is dedicated to St Peter. . . .

Esthwaite Water, to the south of Hill Top and Sawrey, is an interesting lake, being the largest mesotrophic lake in England. The term mesotrophic is indicative of the pH, the acidity or alkalinity of the water. Alkaline waters are the most fertile, acidic waters the least. Mesotrophic waters, such as Esthwaite Water, lie between the two, a neutral water, with a limited range of plant and animal life. However, Esthwaite Water's position is such that there is enhanced productiv-ity within the range of creatures that do occur. The lake is set among fertile soils which enrich the streams that feed it. These fertile soils

Esthwaite Water

are fine agricultural land, and the washed-in fertilisers from the land also enrich the lake. In addition, the lake is very shallow, not 50 feet deep, and the temperature-gradients this causes activate the silt layer at the bottom, ensuring the release of nutrients into the water. As a result the sheltered bays formed in the jigsaw-puzzle-shaped lake show excellent plant life. The North Fen is, in fact, a nature reserve. The plant life is not exotic, but a succession of pondweeds, lilies, rushes and sedges, with a backdrop of trees, chiefly alder and birch. The density of plants at the shore, and their graded height, makes the lake ideal for birdlife, the population increasing in winter when the lake, like Windermere, becomes a stop-over on the migration paths.

Esthwaite Water was beloved of Wordsworth: he called it "our little lake", sensing the intimacy that its pastoral surroundings and almost forgotten air offer the visitor even now. For though lacking the grandeur of the mountain lakes, it's smallness makes it more approachable for the human mind. It is a personal favourite. The difference in atmosphere between Esthwaite Water and the northern lakes is also, of course, due to the geology of the area. Esthwaite lies in the lower, softer Silurian Lakeland region. Just north of the lake is the band of limestone that separates the hard, angular hills from this farmland area. The fells can be seen, just a sharp-edged stone's throw away.

Our route skirts the western shore of the lake, keeping to the minor

road as no shore path exists. The road is heading towards Hawkshead where Wordsworth was at school. Wordsworth skated often on frozen Esthwaite Water, maintaining a love of skating even after a friend died at the lake when the ice broke. Hawkshead is a summer honey-pot, a delightful jumble of old cottages preserved from cars, at least, by a large car park. There have always been visitors to Hawkshead. Two centuries ago they came for wood from the gibbet, a sliver of which, if pushed into a tooth, cured toothache.

Our route does not reach Hawkshead, turning westward (left) at (354 969), just after the Esthwaite Lodge Youth Hostel, on to a path signed for High Barn and Grizedale. Luckily, in leaving the lake edge we avoid confrontation with the boggle, a changeling creature with big red eyes. Legend has it that it appears only to the uneducated, though whether it actually sets unknown walkers an IQ test is not stated. It seeks attention, doing nothing worse than frighten the visitor – at which it is apparently very good – and occasionally preceding its appearance with a noise. One description suggests that the noise is that of a cartload of stone being emptied on the road, which would seem to be adequate as an attention-generator.

The track is obvious, left of cottages and up beside the stream through some fine woodland. On the open hill there are two paths, but both lead to High Barn. There signs point out that though there is a public footpath the farm is not a zoo. It must be strange for the owners, and one can imagine their feelings, if people stray from the path on purpose to poke about in their lives. A lane leads to the road at (343 964). Go right and, shortly, left to approach the Grizedale Forest.

The Forestry Commission's holding in Grizedale, the valley of the pigs, is a massive 3,500 hectares. The area was originally afforested, as elsewhere, with the trees being used to support the iron smelters or bloomeries, and so in a sense the present usage is traditional. However, today 88 per cent of the trees are conifer, half of those Sitka spruce. True, there are some Scots pine, but only 12 per cent of the trees are native broad-leaves. It is easy to become hot under the collar, as Wordsworth did, when confronted with regimented ranks of alien conifers. Business is, unfortunately, the name of this land-management game, and it is perhaps as well to seek the positive achievements of the Commission. Their wildlife management policy has assured the survival of red deer, roe deer and red squirrel in the area. Crossbills enjoy the conifer trees and the secluded tarns are a haven for water fowl.

The right of way through the forest is tedious, going south-west to Lawson Park at (317 951), then northward around Crag Head to the road at (317 968). However, a guide map of the forest, produced by the Commission, shows a permitted through-path that runs virtually due west to dramatically reduce the mileage. It is not a complex path, but one mistake does leave the walker awkwardly placed – one conifer looks very like another. It is essential to have the 1:25000 English Lakes South-East Sheet, and to time, if necessary, the legs of the journey. At (342 965) take the left forked road and follow it to (338 964). Here take the right fork to (3335 9660) where a path, not shown on the 1:25000 sheet, goes off just north of west. Follow this to (3310 9665) and go right on the road. Go right at (3315 9680) and left at (3325 9685). This road is now followed across a junction at (327 971) to a path-fork at (326 972). Go left. Go across at the junction at (3245 9710) and take the left fork at (321 970). Now go down to the road at (318 971). Left from here is Brantwood, last home of John Ruskin. Right is Coniston Water.

John Ruskin lived at Brantwood for the last twenty-nine years of his life, dying in 1900 at eighty-one years of age. He had first seen Lakeland as a boy of five and it made a lasting impression. His was a wealthy family – his father was a wine importer, a partner of Domecq of sherry fame – but young John had a strange childhood. One story has it that his only plaything was a bunch of keys. Such a thing may have freed his imagination, but it imprisoned his soul.

A love affair with Adele Domecq, the partner's daughter, was terminated and an unhappy marriage ended with his wife claiming he was impotent. When he arrived at Brantwood he was worn-out, physically and mentally. Towards the end of his life he became an eccentric recluse. Some have even suggested that he was insane.

Brantwood was built by the Rev. Joseph Hudson whose son, the Rev. Charles Hudson, was killed during the descent from the first climb to the Matterhorn's summit. It contains mememtoes of Ruskin, as does the Ruskin museum in Coniston. There is his geologist's hammer and walking stick – and some of his drawings, and pictures he owned. He was many things – philosopher, social scientist, geologist, writer, painter. To each he brought a new dimension, and yet there is not one field in which he is held to be the best – not even one in which, nowadays, he is a household name.

Ruskin was an undergraduate at Oxford in 1836 and remained at the University until he resigned from the Slade professorship. He championed Turner in his definitive book on modern painters, and painted wonderfully himself. His Turneresque "Thirlmere" is superb. He also championed the pre-Raphaelites, even after losing his wife to Millais. His writing is excellent, full of colour and effect like his painting. Though he proposed all sorts of social changes – including the Green Belt and smokeless zones – his writing style never varied. He said of himself later, somewhat unhappily – "All my life I have been talking to the people, and they have listened, not to what I say, but to how I say it: they have cared not for the matter, but only for the manner of my words".

When he came to Brantwood he interested himself in the local geology, becoming eventually something of an expert on rocks and minerals. Even then, however, his interest was different from the norm. He wanted to understand the rocks for their beauty. His was not a scientific geology, but an aesthetic geology – geology as art. It was a worthwhile venture and perhaps the only part of all his work that had a direct connection with Lakeland. Tolstoy said of him that he was one of the most remarkble men who had ever lived, with the quality of being able to "think with the heart".

To Return

From the car park at the head of the lake take the path eastward to the road at (324 981). Go left and bear left at the junction (326 984). Just after this take the well-signed path to Tarn Howes and The Tarns, one of Lakeland's foremost man-made beauty spots. After following the southern short-line, a path going south-east at (333 999) leads through woods to meet the road at (338 992). Turn right and then left twice for Hawkshead, which can be reached either by following the road, or by taking the footpath right at the top of the hill (339 987).

Distances

Link from Esthwaite to Esthwaite Lodge – 2km
Route Esthwaite Lodge to Coniston Water – 8½kms
Return route – 8km

Tarn Howes

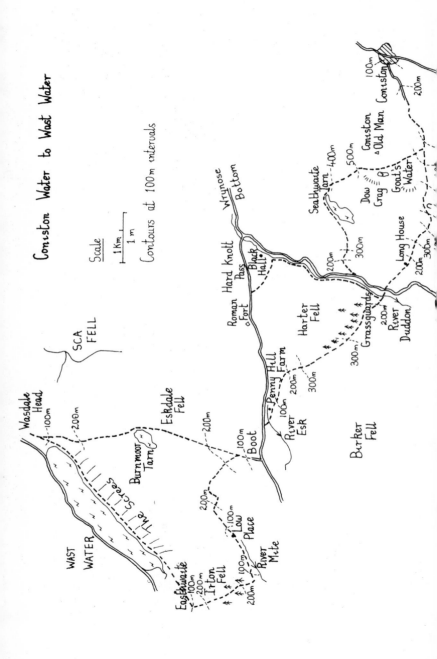

Coniston Water to West Water

Scale

1 Km
1 m

Contours at 100 m intervals

WAST WATER

Wasdale Head
100m
200m

SCA FELL

Screes

Burnmoor Tarn

Eskdale Fell
200m

Eastbrack
100m
200m
Irton Fell
200m
100m
River Mite

100m
Low Place
200m

100m
Boot
River Esk
100m
Penny Hill Farm
200m
300m

Roman Fort

Hard Knott Pass

Wrynose Bottom

Black Hall

Harter Fell
300m

Barker Fell

Grassguards
200m
River Duddon
300m
200m
300m

Long House
200m
300m

Seathwaite
200m
300m
400m
500m

Goat's Water
Dow Crag

Coniston Old Man
Coniston
100m
200m

CONISTON WATER TO WAST WATER

Coniston is third longest of the lakes, and prior to local government changes it could claim to be the largest lake in Lancashire. It is also the lowest of the lakes, the surface being only 105 feet above sea level. Its length and relative quietness were the main considerations when Donald Campbell decided to use it for his attempts on the world water speed record. Campbell's father, Sir Malcolm, had set a record of 142 mph in an early *Bluebird* in 1939. Donald broke this record some sixteen years later with a speed of 202 mph on Ullswater, raising it to 260 mph on Coniston in 1959. On the 4 January 1967 Campbell's last attempt on the record ended when his boat, another *Bluebird*, was travelling at about 328 mph. The nose began to lift into the air and the boat then did a complete backward somersault, breaking up as it hit the lake. The body of the man who had lived for speed and engineering perfection was never found: to this day it rests somewhere in the depths of southern Coniston Water.

The lake was, in earlier times, known as Thurston Water from the Norse god Thor. The name Coniston is not well understood. Probably it means lake-head-town, so possibly this was applied to an

Coniston Water

early settlement before it was used for the lake as well. When viewed from its eastern side, the lake is a magnificent sight, with Coniston Old Man appearing to rise from the village itself. The Old Man is not a reference to some ancient inhabitant of the area but is derived from the Celtic *maen* a pile of stones – and old from *allt* – highest. Strictly speaking the Old Man is, therefore, just the summit cairn. Although not on our route, the summit of the Old Man, at 2631 feet, is well worth the effort to reach and provides magnificent views out to sea and right into the heart of Lakeland. Author Arthur Ransome probably has the distinction of being the youngest person ever to be on this summit of the Coniston Fells, since it is recorded that he was taken there by his father when he was just four weeks old. We are not told of his initial reaction to the view of Coniston Water, which was later to become the setting of his most successful book, *Swallows and Amazons*.

Coniston was once two hamlets, Monk and Church, to distinguish that owned by Furness Abbey from that administered by the church. Despite being Christian institutions they did not always see eye to eye. The combined village is reached by a courtesy path from the lakeside car park, passing over Yewdale Beck. In the waters of this drowned Barbara, maid to Lady Eva Fleming of the local noble family, who was kidnapped by Girt Will, a local giant. Pursued by Barbara's lover and his friends, Girt Will threw her into the beck. Her lover dived after her, and both were drowned. Girt Will was caught by the pursuing gang and, despite his giant's club, was cut to pieces. So violent was his death that there was not enough unslashed skin to make a tobacco pouch – which would certainly have been an eccentric, not to say disgusting, present.

On leaving Coniston, our tour of Lakeland changes character markedly. Up to this point the walk has been through pleasant woods and pastures, but the next stage of our journey takes us across to Wasdale Head, at the heart of the highest mountains in England. And even if the route we are taking keeps particularly to rather lower ground and makes full use of the fellside passes, the change in terrain is immediately clear.

Our first objective is the river Duddon, running through Dunner-dale, one of the least frequented valleys in the area. As a reminder of how timeless this stage of our journey is we could use, as guide, the words of Wordsworth from his 1835 book – "At the head of Coniston

Water there is an agreeable inn, from which an enterprising Tourist might go to the Vale of the Duddon, over Walna Scar, down to Seathwaite, Newfield and the rocks where the river issues from a narrow pass into a broad Vale." The route leaves the main road rightward on the southern side of the hump-back bridge in the centre of the village. Car drivers who wish to return this way may take cars along the first half mile of the route. A few yards up out of the main street, the road passes under an old railway bridge, the first of many reminders on our route of the identical heritage of this part of the National Park.

The road climbs steeply, and one senses the approach of the higher fells with excitement, regardless of the number of previous visits. At the walker's back there are magnificent views over Coniston Water and beyond to the flatter, afforested hills. The road finally gives up, amid a welter of unofficial car parks and we follow a well defined track, which was in earlier times used for quarry traffic. Some of the quarries, particularly those nearer to Coniston, are still in operation, though the scale of operations is now much reduced.

The Walna Scar road that we are following is an old packhorse road, an obvious highway to the western dales which pre-dates even

The Walna Scar road

the quarries. The name is from the Walna Scar spur to the south of Dow Crag, which the path crosses about 2 miles from Seathwaite. From the road, given reasonably clear conditions, the sea in Morecambe Bay can be seen.

There are still rights of way across the Bay sands marked on the Ordnance Survey maps, but to stray can be extremely hazardous. Better, perhaps to use a guide – there are still some who are paid by the Duchy of Lancaster the grand salary of £15 a year. The sea views from Walna Scar might have been very different had George Stephenson proceeded with plans to carry the main Scottish railway across the Bay on a bridge. And they may be different in future if more recent suggestions to dam the Bay to form a freshwater reservoir for south Lancashire became reality.

To the right of our route the Coniston Fells rear up, the outcrops of Dow Crag being high above as the summit of the Scar is approached. In misty conditions the effect can be quite impressive. Our first Lakeland pass is at 1950 feet and is an unmistakable spot, a clear col.

In one of Wordsworth's Duddon sonnets, a collection published in 1820, he wrote of the Duddon Valley – "And desolation is thy patron Saint". Wordsworth also wrote a long poem "The Excursion" about Wonderful Walker, an eighteenth century vicar of the valley village of Seathwaite. Robert Walker was from a poor family, one of twelve children, and after surviving a rather sickly childhood he became a teacher at Loweswater, before taking Holy Orders. He became Vicar of Seathwaite, where he remained for sixty-nine years until his death. On appointment his stipend was £5 a year – it rose to £17 a year by the time he died. Walker is remembered for his kindness to all the villagers. He helped with the various farm tasks and gave financial assistance, despite his own limited income on which he had to support eight children. He died at the age of ninety and his epitaph in the burial register notes that "He was a man singular for his temperance, industry and integrity". The puzzle was that he left £2000, a vast sum in those days, and rather more than his aggregate earnings!

From the col the road goes diagonally across the fell, then follows Longhouse Gill to Long House (238 969). Go left up the lane and right at the top. At (235 968) follow the lane right to an unfenced "village green". Here a beautiful slate gateway allows access to a field, left. Go diagonally across to the footbridge (233 973) that crosses Tarn Beck. Go over the rough ground ahead to (231 975) where there is a signed path to the River Duddon.

In the Duddon Valley

Our route crosses the Duddon, using stepping stones and a wire hawser handrail. The Duddon rises in the vicinity of the Three Shires Stone at the head of Wrynose Pass, and the growing river gathers water from Crinkle Crags. It is an indication of the topographical complexity of this bit of Lakeland that most of the Crinkle's water flows into the Esk, which meets the sea many miles from the mouth of the Duddon.

Beyond the river the immediate target now is the col between Harter Fell and Crook Crag, reached by following Grassguards Gill back up to the fell. Beyond the col, at (206 998) the path splits. Take the left fork, that descends diagonally to Penny Hill Farm (193 007). From the farm a lane leads to the main Eskdale road at (189 009), crossing the Esk over Doctor Bridge. At the road go left and along the road to the signed turn for Boot.

Boot itself is almost the epitome of a Lakeland hamlet. Described as the capital of Eskdale, it preserves several features of interest from

The road to Boot

the last century including the pack-horse bridge, the old mill by the stream and a very quaint street. In addition there is, nearby, the terminus of the railway that runs to the coast at Ravenglass. Originally built to take iron ore away from the valley, it now brings visitors into it.

Parliament granted a bill for the construction of the Ravenglass and Eskdale railway in 1873 and it opened two years later. It was built to a three foot gauge, and was for freight only, but during the first eight months of operation it carried only 6,378 tons of iron ore – a disappointing total – so the following year passenger services were provided for the first time. Not much thought was given to the convenience of the passengers, since there were no toilets at stations and no intermediate stops. Perhaps predictably, the first year of passenger travel was also disappointing and the company had not, even by then, made sufficient profit to pay the builder. By 1877 it had collapsed. For a time, while operated by the receiver, the railway's prospects seemed a little brighter, but by 1884 the mine had closed and the line had really lost its purpose. It was kept open carrying tourists and granite from the Eskdale quarries until the turn of the century. The fifteen inch gauge was adopted in 1915 and from then

The Ravenglass and Eskdale Railway

The road to Burnmore Tarn

on the line ran on enthusiasm and hardwork. The present operators bought it in 1958 against keen competition from scrap metal dealers.

The walker can hear the steam locos beginning their journey to Ravenglass as he begins the next and final stage of the journey to Wast Water. Indeed, for the next half hour or so there is little else on which to focus one's thoughts, because this section of our route is not among the finest parts of the Lakeland tour – although today's walk is going to culminate in magnificence. Leave Boot by crossing the packhorse bridge at the end of the street and bear right to go through a gate. The path from here is well-defined: after reaching open land it just seems to go on and on, although in reality this section of the route is only about five miles in total to Wasdale. It used to be one of the corpse routes of the area, and it is not difficult to imagine mourning groups carrying corpses along it. One local story tells of a horse and cart carrying the body of a young man which disappeared in mist. Shortly afterwards the man's mother died, and the same thing happened again. The son's coffin was subsequently found, but there was never any trace of the mother. So maybe readers would keep an eye open on this part of the walk . . .

Burnmoor Tarn is eventually reached: a lonely spot with a lodge that could certainly be termed a detached property. This spot, at 830 feet, seems to be miles from anywhere, and yet we are only a few hundred yards from the ridge which heralds the descent into Wasdale, Lakeland's most dramatic valley. Straight ahead as the col is crossed lies Great Gable, with Kirkfell and the Pillar Group to the left. To our right is Scafell and Scafell Pike, England's highest summit. The famous Screes, which contribute so much to the well known view down Wasdale, are not in view at this point, being below to our left. The remainder of the path down to the head of the valley is straightforward but well worth taking slowly so that full attention can be given to some of England's grandest scenery. Small wonder this view before us is the symbol of the Lake District National Park.

To Return

As this section of the route is rather long, some may prefer to divide it into sections with breaks in the Duddon valley and at Boot.

Wasdale Head to Boot: Do not allow yourself to be tempted by the footpath marked on the Ordnance Survey maps along the foot of the

screes of Ilgill Head on the south-east side of Wast Water. From either end it looks harmless and inviting, but then, in the words of the great Wainwright, "there comes a vicious quarter-mile compared with which the top of Scafell Pike is like a bowling green". If you cannot resist the temptation, then at least be warned, and allow two to three hours for the three miles along the shore.

But really there is no sensible alternative to following the road along the other (north-west) side of the lake. You will find it pleasant enough as it is mostly unfenced with plenty of springy turf on both sides. Continue beyond the end of the lake and Wasdale Hall Youth Hostel to Woodhow farm (140 042). Here take the footpath to the left, then across the river Irt and to Easthwaite (137 034). Now take the path south to (133 030) where a path leads off south-east through the forest and over Irton Fell. Descend through Miterdale Forest to (142 011). Here turn left and follow the track to Low Place (155 017) and the River Mite. Now follow the river to (162 914) where a path follows Black Gill to White Moss. Descend to Boot.

Boot to Duddon Valley: from Boot go down to the Eskdale road and follow this to the Hard Knott fort (219 014) and the pass itself. Take the path, right, that follows the forest edge before heading north to Black Hall (239 012). Now go south to the River Duddon and follow it to the stepping stones of the outward route.

Duddon Valley to Coniston: Retrace the river walk above to (234 984). Go up to the road, cross it and take the path to Seathwaite Tarn. From the Tarn's eastern end go south and up to Goat's Hawse (266 982). Descend to Goat's Water and follow the path to the Walna Scar road, which is followed to Coniston.

Distances

Route from Coniston Water to Wasdale Head – 24km
  (9km to Duddon Valley, 17km to Boot)
Return Wasdale to Boot – 16km
  Boot to Duddon Valley –12km
  Duddon Valley to Coniston –12km

Wast Water to Ennerdale Water to Buttermere

Scale

1 Km

1 m

Contours at 100m intervals

WAST WATER TO ENNERDALE WATER AND BUTTERMERE

Once we have reached water level the full majesty of Wasdale is apparent. It is wild and desolate, the desolation accentuated by the screes on the south-eastern side of the lake, dropping some 1,800 feet in about 500 yards. To the east are the highest of the fells, though from here Scafell Pike is not dominant, being set well to the side of the valley's head.

The name Wasdale is probably derived from the two Norse words *vatn*, water and *dalr* meaning dale. On the same derivation *wast* water would be water water! The lake is three miles long and half a mile wide, nestling beneath the appropriately named High Screes. The screes continue beneath water level for another 200 feet: Wast Water is the deepest of the lakes with a maximum depth of 254 feet. It is perhaps the most mountain-set of the lakes, with the purest water, but – strangely – it has little by way of plant or fish life because of a lack of nutrients.

It is generally agreed that Wasdale was where British rock-climbing began. But when? In 1886 W.P. Haskett-Smith climbed

Wastwater

Napes Needle, a pinnacle of Great Gable. He climbed the pinnacle alone, an amazing performance. But Haskett-Smith was a remarkable man: to illustrate the point he repeated the climb to mark its jubilee, fifty years later at the age of seventy-four. While the climb is not difficult by modern climbing standards, the seventy-four year olds who complete it must form a very select band.

Haskett-Smith's climb is recognised as the first British rock-climb, but another, earlier, climb is recorded in a letter from the climber to a lady friend, a letter started at Scafell's summit – "surely the first letter ever written from the top of Sca Fell" – and continued after the epic climb. The climb was, in fact, inadvertent, but the fact of its happening and the climber are deeply significant. The date was 2nd August 1802, the climber Samuel Taylor Coleridge.

Coleridge records his rocky descent – it is generally accepted that he descended Broad Stand, now classified as a moderate rock climb, but formidable enough for a first, and solo, climb – in an evocative narrative. He met a "dead sheep quite rotten" that was clearly an omen of what could happen even to the surest of foot. At one stage he feared he was trapped, being unable to go back up and afraid of the sheer wall below him, and lay down to calm his trembling body.

But Coleridge negotiated the drop and made it to the base of the rocks. He was uplifted – "O how I wished for Health and Strength that I might wander about for a Month together, in the stormiest month of the year, among these places, so lonely and savage and full of sounds". Coleridge was ahead of his time in his attitude to the hills, he was the first backpacker, he used nailed boots a full century before they were popular, and he soloed mountains and rock-climbs when most just viewed them from afar, and that still with trepidation.

Today Coleridge's arrival in Lakeland is seen as heralding the Age of the Lake Poets, rather than the Age of the Rock Climber.

The Wasdale Head Hotel was to cater "for the idiots who walk the hills", in the words of Will Ritson who built it. Ritson was a local man who had a variety of unconventional ideas. In the case of the hotel however, his assessment of the potential was realistic and "the idiots" have turned up in sufficient numbers ever since to ensure its continuing success. Ritson was also a wonderful tall-story teller. He was given the title of World Champion Liar, but offered to resign it in favour of a visiting bishop who claimed never to have told a lie. One day at his inn he told a group of ladies the harrowing tale of a family including six children who forced their way homewards to their lonely farm on the fell against blizzards and cold. At a freezing stream they one by one were swept away to their deaths. The ladies cried, and Will reassured them. It might have been worse, he said. How? they cried. Well, he said, it might have been true.

Our next objective is the wooded valley of Ennerdale, just over the ridge from Wasdale, a ridge containing a selection of some of Lakeland's finest peaks. The short journey between the valleys begins behind the hotel, going over the fine slate pack-horse bridge and following, at first, the deep valley of Mosedale. There are paths on both sides of the Mosedale beck: the path leading to the Black Sail pass is to the right. To the right are the slopes of Kirk Fell, a conical sister to Great Gable beyond. Opposite Kirk Fell are the screes coming down from Red Pike. Names become a little confusing at this point: there are a number of duplicated names in Lakeland but this Red Pike is only about three miles as the high-level crow flies from Red Pike of Buttermere. In addition, both are fairly prominent peaks. Wasdale's version is 2,629 feet, and its Buttermere namesake is only slightly lower, at 2,479 feet. The Red Pike above the screes is part of the Pillar-Steeple group of fells which offer fine walking. The Black Sail path rises up the flanks of Kirk Fell, but follows a beautifully graded route, a reminder that this is an old trading route over which slate was carried to Coniston from the quarries above Honister. As the path gains height it is possible fully to appreciate the dry stone walling in Wasdale below. The earliest walls in this part of Lakeland were probably built by the monks of Furness Abbey. They were not constructed from quarried slates but from the cobbles gathered from the clearing of the ground for cultivation. The well-built dry stone wall is basically two walls, constructed in much the same way as a modern cavity wall, except that the cavity is filled with rubble, adding to the wall's strength. Further strength is obtained by bridging stones, coupling the two walls.

The path climbs gently to the head of the pass at a height of around 1,750 feet, and there the vast Ennerdale forest comes in to view. Many writers have bemoaned the afforestation of Ennerdale, and certainly it has changed, but the valley in its present state is by no means unattractive. The forest stretches about six miles, from the head of the valley to the lower end of the violin-shaped lake, still out of sight from the pass. This forest, planted in the earlier part of the twentieth century, was not the first Ennerdale Forest.

In medieval times much of the land which was not under the control of the Furness monks was designated as forest, though not in the sense of the present forest. A forest at that time was a royal hunting ground, and though it might include areas of woodland it might also include areas of open heath or moor. The area was protected from anyone who might threaten the hunting by enclosing and cultivating land. The forest here probably consisted of scrubby woodland providing shelter for deer, wolves and wild boars. As the local population grew and the old forest law was relaxed, increasing areas of land came under cultivation. The last refuge of the red deer in the area was to the south-east of Ennerdale Water on the hillside known as "The Side", a remnant of the original forest under the ownership of the Furness monks since 1338. Even today the slopes to the south of the lake have a fine collection of ash, oak, and birches with a carpet of mosses.

The opportunity to take a closer look into the Ennerdale valley, including a walk around the lake, comes after descending from the Black Sail pass and crossing the river Liza, the river which rises between Great Gable and Green Gable, and flows into Ennerdale Water. After passing the Black Sail Youth Hostel, surely one of the most remote hostels in the country (it is six miles from the nearest road) the route to Buttermere bears right, up the hill, over the Scarth Gap Pass; but to reach Ennerdale Water, carry straight on, joining the forest road. Just before reaching the top of the lake, another youth hostel, Ennerdale, is situated by the road side. It is slightly more comfortable than its neighbour by the head of the valley, but it, too, is in a remote and peaceful location.

Continue along the forest track, around the head of the lake, eventually crossing a small dam – a reminder that Ennerdale has been a reservoir for Whitehaven since 1947. In the early sixties there were plans to raise the water level by four feet, but they were shelved. If they had not been, our footpath back to the head of the lake would have been submerged. After the short ascent to Robin Hood's Chair on Angler's Crag, the view makes the excursion around the lake a worthwhile extension to the main walk. Much of the remainder of the shore line path is rocky, and some care is needed, though the ground

Ennerdale from Scarth Gap

becomes easier towards the head of the lake, where a left turn is made to cross the Liza, rejoin the forest road and retrace our steps back towards the Scarth Gap Path.

The route to the Scarth Gap pass is straightforward, and above the tree-line the views towards Ennerdale Water and across the valley to Pillar are excellent. At the pass head an old gate stands lonely and forlorn. For many years there has been no fence on either side, and recently the gate collapsed from its posts. Go through, round or over the gate and on to the top of the slope to Buttermere. To the right there is Haystacks, perhaps the most distinctive and picturesque of all the Lakeland peaks. It is little wonder that it is so frequently climbed.

The path to Buttermere is easy, though steep at its lower end, and allows a good view of the long valley running back from the Honister Pass, with its three lakes.

To Return

There is no easy way from Buttermere to Wast Water other than to reverse the outward route. An alternative is to do the route in two sections from one of the Ennerdale car parks.

Scarth Gap

Buttermere to Ennerdale Water: from Buttermere village take the path across Scale Bridge (168 166) to Scale Force (150 172). Now go west along the obvious track to the ridge across Black Beck (146 173). A less well-defined route now crosses the head of Mosedale and Floutern Cap on barren fell. Follow the Gill Beck valley down to the road at (101 165). Here go right, left at the road junction and along the path at (098 166). Or go left along the road. These routes lead to the lake car parks.

Ennerdale Water to Wast Water: from either car park at Ennerdale follow the lake path to (134 141). Go over the River Liza and follow Woundfell Beck and then Deep Gill up to the col (149 109) between Haycock and Scoot Fell. From here a path follows Nether Beck to Wast Water.

Distances

Route from Wast Water to Buttermere – 10km
(extension to Ennerdale Water from Black Sail Hut – 16km)
(circumnavigation of Ennerdale water – 10km).
Return: Buttermere to Ennerdale Water – 12km. Ennerdale Water to Wast Water – 15km.

Buttermere from Scarth Gap

Waterend

Darling Fell

LOWESWATER

Holme Wood

Loweswater

High Park

Mellbreak

Grasmoor

CRUMMOCK WATER

Scale Force

Newlands

Buttermere

Buttermere Fell

Red Pike

BUTTERMERE

High Stile

High Crag

Buttermere,
Crummock Water
and Loweswater

1Km
1m   Scale

BUTTERMERE, CRUMMOCK WATER AND LOWESWATER

The Buttermere valley is less remote than Wasdale and Ennerdale, it even has easy access from Keswick and Cockermouth. Yet despite this, it retains its own special charms and seems strangely isolated from the rest of Lakeland.

Its most obvious unusual feature is the presence of three lakes, Buttermere, Crummock Water and Loweswater. The first two are separated by only a narrow, flat strip of land less than a mile wide, and it is little surprise to discover that they were, in fact, once joined as a single lake. The deposits which today separate them were brought down as silt by Sail Beck, from the slopes of Eel Crag and Whiteless Pike.

But while two of the lakes clearly have a common origin – a fact which becomes even more obvious in times of flood – Loweswater is very different. It seems almost isolated, nestling between the fells like a low-level, slightly overgrown, tarn.

The Loweswater end of the valley is on Skiddaw slate and it is this rock which gives the north-eastern side of the valley its smooth slopes. The continuity of the slopes is interrupted only by the Sail Beck valley, which now carries the road towards Newlands Pass. In sharp contrast, the head of the valley, below Fleetwith Pike, and the south-western slopes, has faces fretted by a number of corries, because while the lower levels are still made up of the Skiddaw slates, these merge with the volcanic rocks of the Borrowdale series.

To visit Loweswater (above which once lived Crutchey, a crippled thief who had a shoe fitted the wrong way round on the end of his crutch to confuse pursuers), leave Buttermere village past the Fish Hotel. This was once the home of Mary Robinson (Mary of Buttermere) whose romance with a man who turned out to be a bigamist defrauder has been related in a significant proportion of the many books on Lakeland. What is less well-known than the basic facts are that Captain Joseph Budworth mentioned Mary first in an article in 1792, thus creating the reputation that was her downfall. Later all the Lakeland poets visited her, and Wordsworth also visited James Hatfield, the bigamist fraud, in Carlisle jail. Hatfield was actually tried only on three counts of forgery totalling £50; Mary Robinson was not called as a witness and the bigamy charge was not made. It was thought that the jury of locals, and the judge, would have been lenient had it not been for Mary, by the time of Hatfield's arrest, expecting his child. The judge claimed that "crimes of such magnitude as have seldom, if ever, received any mitigation of capital punishment", which is not exactly the truth. In the manner of the day the newspapers covered, minute by minute, Hatfield's last hour. He read the *Carlisle Journal*, drank coffee, shaved, dined and so on. He met the executioner and gave him money. He wore "fustion pantaloons", said "O, a happy sight – I see it with pleasure" on viewing the gallows, tied his own blindfold and that's enough of that.

Woods near Crummock Water

Winding its way across the delta, our path reaches Buttermere Dubbs, the deep clear waterway between the twin lakes. Cross by the pack-horse bridge, which gives an excellent excuse for a stopping place, not through need, as the terrain so far is about as easy as possible, but to contemplate the views across the head of Crummock Water, a more elegant lake than Buttermere. Across the lake from here, on a small island, there always seem to be three cormorants standing sentinel like the ghostly birds from the lighthouse-disaster story. The path now becomes somewhat more rocky and heads up to Scale Force (150 170), at 120 feet one of Lakeland's highest waterfalls. The falls are somewhat off our route but worth the detour, especially in very windy weather when the water sheet is dispersed as

a spray. The descent from the waterfall crosses the beck to meet the western shore of Crummock Water at (157 179). The navigation from this point is straightforward, following a path that rises gently up the fell, to Highpark (145 202), from where a lane leads to Loweswater village. (It is perhaps a little odd that the village takes the name of the smaller of two lakes from which it is about equidistant.) From the village go north to the road (141 211) and then left. At (138 211) a footpath goes south-west to the lake edge at Holme wood. The wood is for the most part a natural wood, only the upper part being newly afforested, and contains a collection of mature trees. It is owned by the National Trust, in common with much of the Buttermere valley. After crossing the beck, which works its way down a series of delightful waterfalls collectively called Holme Force, the path soon leaves both the wood and the lake behind. Pass Hudson Place (116 222) and join the road at (118 225) near the aptly named Waterend.

A couple of miles road walking is now inevitable, the only alternative requiring the ascent of Darling and Low Fells. Beyond Loweswater village, cross the river Cocker then turn right (149 216) along the path through Lanthwaite wood, meeting the Buttermere

Above Buttermere

road beneath the crags of Grasmoor End (160 200). From here follow the road back to Buttermere. From the road the lake is imposing rather than picturesque, despite the post-card views.

Distance

Tour of Buttermere, Crummock Water and Loweswater – 20km. If the tour of Loweswater is dropped in favour of just reaching that lake, this decreases it to 16km.

Buttermere to Derwent Water

Scale

1 Km

1 m

Contours at 100m intervals

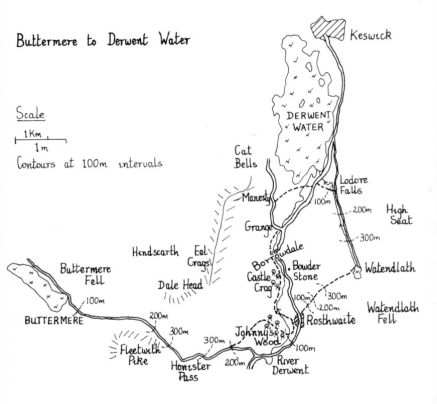

Keswick

DERWENT
WATER

Cat
Bells

Manesty

100m

Lodore
Falls

200m

High
Seat

Grange

300m

Hindscarth

Eel
Crags

Borrowdale

Bowder
Stone

Castle
Crag

Watendlath

Buttermere
Fell

Dale Head

100m

200m

Rosthwaite

Watendlath
Fell

BUTTERMERE

100m

200m

300m

Johnny's
Wood

300m

300m

Fleetwith
Pike

Honister
Pass

200m

100m

River
Derwent

BUTTERMERE TO DERWENT WATER

Honister was the scene of a legendary battle when the Grahams, Scot's raiders, were ambushed after raiding Borrowdale. They were slaughtered, their war chief buried beneath a cairn on Hindscarth, and the rest under two flat and lettered stones that anciently lay beside the second bridge.

Honister: "The scene was terrifying; not an herb to be seen, but wild savine growing in the interstices of the naked rocks; the horrid projection of vast promontories, the vicinity of the clouds, the thunder of the explosions in the slate quarries, the dreadful solitude, the distance of the plain below, and the mountains heaped on mountains that were piled around us, desolate and waste like the ruins of a world we have survived, excited such ideas of horror as are not to be expressed."

Honister, Pass and Crag, has always excited emotion. Even the lack of a satisfactory explanation for the name enhances the mystery of a place that can be dark and foreboding if the weather is a touch malevolent. The quotation above is from the first half of the eighteenth century when the quarries at the head of the pass were in full production. Today there is still slate working, with the inevitable craft centre.

Many will consider it inappropriate that any walking route through Lakeland should choose to go via Honister, since a road goes that way. But our route seeks passes, and this is the finest in the area. The car-tourist must not be allowed to have it all to himself. Honister is the best of Lakeland passes, the walls being both long, high and rocky. The approach from Buttermere is Lakeland compressed into a few miles: the lake, the rocky peaks of Haystacks and Fleetwith Pike, the long rugged pass, the entry into a dale. The dale is Borrowdale, probably the most famous of all Lakeland dales, a name synonymous with the beauty of Lakeland.

To enter Borrowdale our route crosses the Honister pass. In the lower reaches it is easy to stay away from the road, following the stream and absorbing the local view of Honister Crag and the ridge of Hindscarth Edge. Towards the top of the pass, as the Hawse is approached, it is more difficult to avoid the tarmac. So be careful.

The view that opens up as Honister Hawse is topped makes the following of a road worthwhile. Descend towards Borrowdale and look for an old road that leaves the tarmac road to the left at (236 138). Our route does not actually follow this road, which meanders down the dale side to Seatoller, but follows the left side of a wall reached at (242 142). Cross a wall running left to right by a stile. The stream here is Scaleclose Gill, and we are making for a waterfall on it, but no footpath follows it here, the route going on for another 300 yards, hugging the wall to the right. There is a quick glimpse of Derwent Water, and then a path goes off right, heading down to Scaleclose Force and Johnny Wood. This fine woodland – all the woodland in Borrowdale is excellent – is traversed to the hamlet of Longthwaite. The River Derwent is crossed by a footpath that leads through to Rosthwaite – *hross-thwaite*, the clearing of the horse.

From Rosthwaite a footpath, at (247 148), leads back westward to the Derwent again where there is a ford to the west bank, or a path on the east can be followed. Either way go north to the New Bridge (252 152). Now follow the obvious path on the Derwent west bank to the

Honister Pass

woodland of Castle Crag. A square mile of countryside centred slightly north of Castle Crag is, according to Wainwright (and who, therefore, would argue?) the loveliest square mile in Lakeland. It is a good spot to contemplate Borrowdale. Wainwright's square mile, as he himself points out, contains no mountain, lake or famous crag. It does hold the Bowder Stone, a monolith that Thomas West maintained had a solidity of 23,090 feet, whatever that means. Today the stone is much visited, the handrails of the steps to its top are worn smooth by hands, the steps worn rough by feet. Some say the stone is named for Baldar, son of Odin, but it is more likely to be named from *bield*, a temporary shelter used by shepherds. Neither Baldar nor the shepherds would be thrilled by the white chalk marks left by the newest generation of rock climbers.

The name of Borrowdale itself is better understood. It is from the dale of the *burgh*, or hill fort. The hill fort in question stands on the tree-lined top of Castle Crag. The Crag dominates the Jaws of Borrowdale, creating a defenceable valley. The valley was never rich enough to offer an easy living, but perhaps safety was more important than a full stomach. Gilpin notes that "this valley, so replete in hideous grandeur, is known by the name of the Straits of Borrowdale. In this deep retreat lies the village of Rosthwaite, having at all times little intercourse with the country; but during half the year, almost totally excluded from all human commerce". The people lived on "scanty patches of arable land" which they "cultivated with difficulty".

The wheeled cart did not reach Borrowdale until 1750 when it replaced the horse-drawn sled. Conditions were harsh, the dale folk appearing to spend their whole year either preparing for, or living through, the winters. If winter was early, or lasted late, the effect was disastrous. Around its coming grew a legend of twelve silent men who sat around a fire. Three wore cloaks of green (the grass), three wore gold (the ripe corn), three wore red (the leaves of autumn) and three wore white (the snow). The men poked the fire (the sun) in turn, but if one fell asleep and missed his turn the weather missed a beat and savaged the crops and dale folk.

The isolation of the dale, and the lack of worldliness that it gave the dale folk, allowed innumerable stories to grow up about their gullibility. It was said that one year, knowing that the cuckoo came in spring and stayed until summer's end, they decided to keep the bird in the

dale, to ensure that summer too would never go. So they built a wall across the valley entrance to keep in the gowk, the local word for a cuckoo, but sadly it flew over the top. After this tale the dale folk were known as gowks. Another story has a mule arriving in the valley and being shown to the local wise man by incredulous gowks. The wise man contemplated it for a long time. He knew it was not a horse, or a donkey, or a few other animals he was familiar with. It must be something of which he had heard but which he had never seen. He decided, at length, that it was a peacock.

In the quarries below Castle Crag lived Millican Dalton, the self-styled Professor of Adventure, the last (or latest) in a long line of Derwent Water hermits, who died within living memory. Dalton lived the simple life, making his own clothes and walking equipment. He was not a tramp, neither did he believe in the hair-shirt. He owned an eiderdown. He was a mountain guide, charging no fee but requesting something towards his frugal needs and strict vegetarian diet.

Our route traverses Wainwright's loveliest mile through the National Trust woodland on the west bank of the Derwent. As the wood finishes, at (250 170), a path leads direct into Grange-in-Borrowdale. This lovely hamlet was a 12th century granary for the monks of Furness Abbey. They also collected salt from a saline spring. Today it is a quiet hamlet frequently made noisy by tourists crossing the lovely double arched bridge over the Derwent.

It was to Grange that Thomas Gray came in 1769, the first of many poets drawn to the area. Gray, most famous for his "Elegy", made his tour, sadly, only a year before he died. It is sad, not only because of the loss to English literature of the time, but because Gray had rediscovered, in Scotland only four years before, a love of the country in general and mountains in particular. The dalefolk were in good spirits, recounting the plundering of a golden eagle's eyrie. Such vandalism (rightly) takes our breath away, but at that time the dale-folk believed that the eagles, with their appetite for young lambs as well as game-birds, were considerable competitors.

Thomas Gray dined at Grange on cold tongue, oat cakes and butter washed down with milk. At Lodore the crags reminded him of something told him by a guide in Swizterland: he should "move with speed and say nothing lest the agitation of the air should loosen the snows above and bring down a mass that would overwhelm a caravan.

I took this counsel here and hastened on in silence". Poor Gray has been much mocked by later writers for his nervousness (in 1787 James Clarke claimed that he was so timid that when he saw Skiddaw he quickly pulled down the blinds of his carriage – a story which seems to have been invented). Gray was a mild and timid man, and his description of Lakeland leaves the reader in no doubt that climbing mountains was not for him; but he was unaccustomed to them, and loud noises *can* trigger avalanches, so a rather extreme reaction to Lodore's crags is not impossible. In the mid-eighteenth century people were very ready to see uncontrolled nature as raw and terrifying.

Thomas West, author of the first true guide to Lakeland, had little patience with such notions. He refers to Gray's descriptions of Honister and Borrowdale as ". . . the hyperboles; the sport of fancy he was pleased to indulge himself in." West's book is still an excellent read for anyone interested in late eighteenth-century Lakeland. It starts: "Since persons of genius, taste and observation, began to make the tours of their own country, and to give such pleasing accounts of the natural history, and improving state of the northern parts of the kingdom, the spirit of visiting them has diffused itself among the curious of all ranks." It is reassuring to learn that we need no longer be Top People to enjoy Lakeland.

The Salt Well is marked on the 1:25000 leisure sheet and our route heads towards it, and Manesty, along the minor road. At (251 183) a footpath, signed "Lodore", leads off north-east to the southern tip of Derwent Water. This path is easily followed, if for no other reason than because the way forward can be seen across the flat water meadows, crossing the Derwent by the bridge at (260 187), to reach the B5289 – the main road in Borrowdale – at (263 187). North from here, at (266 196) is a cark park, where the shore of the lake can be reached.

Derwent Water vies with Bassenthwaite for being the fourth biggest Lakeland lake: experts disagree which is actually the larger after Windermere and Coniston Water, that we have already passed, and Ullswater, still to come. Like Windermere, it is studded with islands, the largest of which, St Herbert's, is named from a famous hermit. The Venerable Bede writes all that is known of St Herbert in his life of St Cuthbert, the famous Bishop of Lindisfarne. The two

men were friends and when Cuthbert told Herbert that he was dying, Herbert begged to be allowed to go with him to heaven. Cuthbert prayed again and was told that the wish had been granted. He told Herbert, who left joyfully to return to his island home. The two men died later, within an hour of each other.

Locally St Herbert was famous, and his island was a place of pilgrimage. In the 14th century services were held on the island in celebration of the saint's life, and anyone attending the service received forty days of indulgence. Perhaps the last, and best, word on St Herbert was written by Camden, who claimed that the saint had lived "an Hermeticall Life" which might go some way towards explaining its purity.

Near where we stand, in the south-eastern corner of the lake, there appears from time to time a floating island. This was once considered legendary, but is now a firmly established fact, the explanation being the raising of a mass of vegetation by methane gas. At times there have been as many as three islands at once. Jonathan Otley investigated one of them in the early 19th century, deciding that it was six feet thick with a layer of vegetable matter on a clay and peat soil. In 1857 Postlethwaite landed on the island, standing on a plank laid across it. Since then there have been other landings, including a group of girl guides who raised a Union Jack and claimed the island for England. The guides were lucky. This area of lake is prone to bottom winds that are said to blow so locally that boats within yards of each other experience conditions as different as dead calm and a capsizing squall. Though often exaggerated, the winds are real, probably a result of the mountains creating strange air-pressure distributions.

To Return

From the Hotel near the edge of Derwent Water (262 183), take the path east to Watendlath and go right to the hamlet (275 163). There take the signed path beside the Tarn that follows Bowdergate Gill, and goes over the fell to Resting Stone (264 155) and down into Rosthwaite. From here reverse the route to Honister and Buttermere.

Distances
Route from Buttermere to Derwent Water – 15km
Return route – 16km

Derwent Water to Bassenthwaite Lake

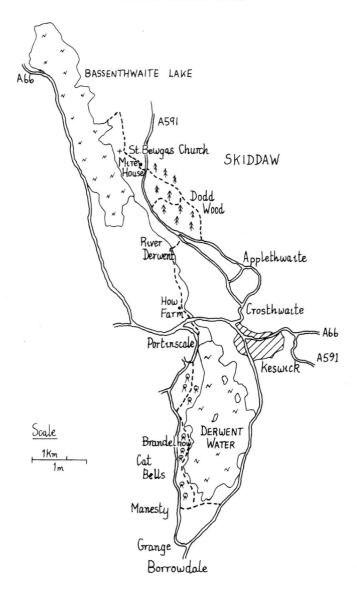

Bassenthwaite Lake

A66

A591

St. Bewgas Church

Mire House

SKIDDAW

Dodd Wood

River Derwent

Applethwaite

How Farm

Crosthwaite

Portinscale

A66

A591

Keswick

Scale

1 Km

1 m

Brandelhow

Cat Bells

DERWENT WATER

Manesty

Grange

Borrowdale

DERWENT WATER TO BASSENTHWAITE LAKE

Bassenthwaite – the name is believed to derive from Bassen's clearing, Bassen presumably being a Norse chieftain – is the only stretch of water in Lakeland that is actually called a lake. It is also inconveniently placed, away from the natural circle of our route. To compensate, the walk towards it, along the western shore of Derwent Water or, alternatively, along the base of the Catbells ridge, is a fine excursion, and allows the possibility of a return around the northern tip of Derwent Water through the town of Keswick.

The route reverses the last stage of that given previously to the point (254 186) where the path towards Manesty, to the left, may be ignored in favour of that back towards Derwent Water, which goes right. The choice is straightforward. The lake walk hugs the shore line through the parkland of Manesty and Bradelhow, giving fine close views of the water. The path is sometimes indistinct, and occasionally damp, but is never difficult to follow. All fences are breached by gates and often the very edge of the lake can be followed. In the right season the woodland is carpeted with bluebells. Wordsworth's daffodils may symbolise Lakeland for many people, but the bluebell is really the Lakeland flower. The "mountain" route leaves the road at Manesty (251 185) to head up the Catbells ridge. At (249 187) the right fork is taken, the walker following the woodland edge and lower slopes of the ridge. Either route arrives at the road at (248 212) where the signed footpath, onto the National Trust land at Hawes End, leads off into the woodland again, to rejoin the road for Portinscale at (252 228).

On the Catbells route, above Brackenburn, near the house at (249 192), the ridge walker can view the lake from a stone seat. This was erected to the memory of Sir Hugh Walpole whose house it was. Sir Hugh was another of the many writers drawn to Lakeland for peace and inspiration. As a boy Walpole had Lakeland holidays, and was particularly fond of the time he had climbed Great Gable to watch the sunrise, was soaked by rain on his descent and had a puncture on his bike going back to the holiday home. He had always loved Derwent Water and Borrowdale, and bought Brackenburn when he was thirty-eight years old and already established as a writer. The house was "stone among the loveliest stone in the world, having a shade of green like a tulip leaf, a purple depth like a bishop's ring and a dove-shadowed grey over all".

His "Rogue Herries" novels drew on the local area, here and Watendlath, and brought him considerable success at the time. He died in 1941 and is buried in Keswick. Today his writing is less fashionable but despite that, as his description of Borrowdale stone above shows, his is a fine prose. He was also an endearing character. How could we disapprove of a man who built extra storeys on Brackenburn as the trees grew so as to keep his views of the lake?

Above Brackenburn, and above the stone seat, is Catbells, perhaps the most popular of all Lakeland fells because of its (relatively) gentle slopes, low height and wonderful views of water and mountain. The name is said to be from cat *bield*, cat's shelter, but this is disputed by those who maintain that the name is not old enough to be a memory of the long-gone wild cat. It does appear that Coleridge, for instance, was not aware of the name. Crags to the west of the summit are known as mart bield, the marten's shelter, and it may be that the marten, probably the pole-cat rather than the pine marten, was lately replaced, in name, by the cat.

Our route enters Portinscale and heads north past the Post Office and Tower Hotel to a superb suspension bridge over the Derwent. Here a footpath, signed "How Farm and Braithwaite Moss" follows the river. The main roads, the B5289 and A76, are underpassed in reaching How Farm. Here do not go to Braithwaite Farm, but take the Allerdale Ramble path that again follows the Derwent to High Stock Bridge (243 260), crossing it to reach the A591 at an unmarked stile (246 263).

The Derwent in this stretch is a sluggish river flowing through poorly drained water meadows. The height difference between Bassenthwaite Lake and Derwent Water is only twenty feet, so there is little driving head.

Go left on the A591 to reach Dancing Gate, and the start of Dodd Wood. Dodd Wood is an aggravation to anyone wanting to get to Bassenthwaite Lake. The path leading to the lake leaves the A591 at (234 281), but that is almost 1 1/2 miles from Dancing Gate. That is a long time to be risking instant annihilation, or longer term lead poisoning. The alternative, of using the permissive paths on the Forestry Commission roads in Dodd Wood, is to be preferred, but there is no road that runs directly from the first permitted entry, at (237 272) to the second entry at (235 282). The problem is Skill Beck which carves a valley that is not crossed except at (237 278), deep in the wood and far up the hillside. And, of course, by the time the first entry is reached you are half way to the path you seek. It is best, perhaps, to settle for the main road, to be careful, and to enjoy the view. A longer, purer alternative would be go to towards Millbeck from Dancing Gate and take the path into the wood at (247 264) where Scalesbeck Gill reaches the road. The forest roads can now be followed, contouring north of Dodd to the northern side of the Skill Beck Valley. It is no great distance, but there is some climbing and a lot of conifers.

The route to the lake is unmarked, though obvious, at (235 281), leading past Mire House and St Bewgas church. From the church follow the edge of Highfield Wood until a path heads off northwards, left, to the road at (266 297). Go left and along the road to (225 298) where a slate-slab marked path leads off to Bowness Bay and Bassenthwaite Lake. This is as far north as we shall go on our journey.

We are a few yards north of Skiddaw summit, and to many the Skiddaw-Blencathra ridge, a great wall of mountain, is the enclosing fence of Lakeland to the north. The National Park goes on for a few more miles as the Uldale and Caldbeck Fells drop down off Skiddaw to the River Caldew, the country of John Peel.

There are still those who are amazed when they discover that there was a real John Peel and that the song so romantically linked with

Skiddaw from Sticks Pass

long-gone, "better" days, whistled by the Light Brigade during their famous Charge, is just another country ballad with a catchy tune. But Peel was real enough, and was hardly a man you would want as your next door neighbour. Born around 1776 to well-off parents, he eloped to Gretna at twenty with the daughter of another well-off farmer. The marriage can hardly have given Mrs Mary Peel much pleasure, though it did give her thirteen children, because – having independent means – Peel was able to spend almost all his time indulging in his favourite pursuits, hunting and drinking. The former appears to have dominated his daylight hours, the latter his nights. He hunted on the day of his son's funeral, and left the house while his wife was giving birth to twins declaring that he did not care if it was four not two, he was off. His drinking sessions were legendary, lasting several days at a time, and his neighbours were often wakened in the early hours by his loud shouting at he staggered home – and also by his habit of blowing his hunting horn at ungodly hours – "For the sound of his horn brought me from my bed" all too often! For many locals he was a rough, aggressive, bullying drunk, yet at his funeral – he died in 1854 – several thousand people turned up. Peel was outlived by his wife, and a good number of his children. One son was "Young John" until his death at ninety-two.

Peel's fame lies in the song written by his friend John Woodcock Groves during one extravagant drinking session. The words were originally set to a traditional air, but were re-set later, after Peel's death. The story of Groves commenting "By Jove, Peel, you shall be sung when we are both run to earth" is a jolly, romantic touch. But Groves was hardly jolly or romantic. He made nothing from the song and seems to have been possessed of an anti-Midas touch. He emigrated to Tasmania in 1833 where he was still a misfit, a failed merchant and failed inventor. He frequently left his wife to go walkabout like an Aborigine, spoke out against flogging yet beat one son so hard he spent three years in bed and was crippled for life, and was locked up in a mental home but escaped to die at the ripe old age of ninety-one.

The pair, Peel in particular, are often seen as "larger-than-life" and "amiable rogues". On the evidence, they were the sort of unsavoury pair most people would be glad to see the back of.

Bassenthwaite Lake is a large stretch of water, well set against Broom Fell, and is said to have inspired Tennyson to write the

"Morte d'Arthur". There is good fen-land at the southern tip, but it is not easily viewed and the lake is little visited by the Lakeland tourist – and yet the weather can be fine here while the central Lakes are being rained upon. In 1780 it is said that a horse race was held in Bassenthwaite. "In", not "on" the lake when frozen, as you might think: a boat-load of horses was towed to the lake centre and scuttled, whereupon the horses raced (that is swam) ashore.

To return to Derwent Water from our visit to Bassenthwaite Lake there is little lowland alternative to reversing the route. The lower Skiddaw fells can be gained from Dodd Wood or, better, the minor road at (244 264) can be followed through Millbeck and Applethwaite – Robert Southey's favourite vantage point – to gain Crosthwaite and then Keswick.

Crosthwaite Church is the oldest, and one of the finest, churches in the area, and is associated with, and dedicated to St Kentigern. Kentigern, also known as Mungo, was the son of Thenew, a nun thrown from a cliff for her sinful pregnancy. The boy was pious almost from birth and, as a member of the Celtic church, came to Cumbria as bishop around 573 AD. He owned no horse or ass, walking throughout his see. He ate only fruit and vegetables, wore a hair shirt and slept on a bed of ashes in a stone coffin. Such asceticism appealed to the locals and he was revered as the Apostle of Strathclyde. He died in 612 AD. Later the church had, as vicar, Canon H.D. Rawnsley, friend of John Ruskin and Beatrix Potter and co-founder of the National Trust.

Bassenthwaite Lake

Keswick is the largest town in north Lakeland – given that Cockermouth lies outside the circle of lake influence – and with its wide centre is a picturesque spot. The name is pronounced without the assistance of the "w", a pronunciation shared with other Lakeland wicks. The wick is from *wic*, dwelling, with *ces* from cheese. This was, originally, a dairy farm. An Elizabethan market charter helped the town's prosperity, but its real establishment came with the metal and wadd mining of Borrowdale. At one time Keswick had several smelters, including the largest silver smelting works in England. The town's industrial phase came to an abupt end when Cromwell's soldiers destroyed the metal smelters to prevent their use in weapon-making.

For some time Keswick was home for Samuel Taylor Coleridge (1772–1834), who shared Greta Hall, near the town, with his fellow Lake Poet, Robert Southey. They had become friends as young men: two radical philosopher-poets who decided to create a new kind of society, to be known as the Pantisocracy, in the new world of America. It would be communal, based on living off the land, poetry and the exchange of ideas, and its first members would be twelve young men and a number – to be decided – of young ladies. One of these would be Edith Fricker, whom Southey planned to marry, and another would be Edith's sister Sara, who became Coleridge's wife – simply, he maintained later, because she was part of the grand American scheme.

When that scheme fell through Coleridge moved to Greta Hall to be near his great friend William Wordsworth. He discovered the hills, and a passionate need for the solitude they offered: "I must be alone, if either my Imagination or Heart are to be enriched". The Mountain Rescue Association would hardly have approved his attitude to his solitary scrambles. "I am too confident and too indolent to look around about till I find a track or other symptom of safety; but I wander on and where it is first possible to descend, there I go – relying upon fortune for how far down this possibility will continue." Of such wanderings the Broad Stand descent, noted near Wasdale, was born.

Eventually the Coleridges, who had had three children, were joined by the Southeys. Southey hoped that his wife would be comforted, after the death of a child, by the company of her sister,

Greta Hall

and Coleridge was ready to welcome anything to relieve the pressure of a failing marriage. His natural impracticality was aggravated by addiction to opium, a result of using laudanum – the "aspirin" of the day – to control the pain of rheumatism and gout, so that he was ill-suited to family responsibilities. Southey, on the other hand – an extremely industrious and responsible man – seems to have been made for them; and an unkind interpretation of Coleridge's enthusiasm for sharing Greta Hall might be that it stemmed from relief at finding a provider for his wife and children and a liberator for himself.

That is how it happened. Southey, who was eventually to have eight children of his own, undertook the support of Sara Coleridge and her three, and of two more of his wife's sisters. It is not surprising that he left his desk for only one hour's brisk walk round Derwent Water each day; and it was lucky that his huge output of written work, almost all of it forgotten today, was highly successful at the time. Meanwhile Coleridge was freed to leave Greta Hall, which he had come to dislike, and make a journey overseas before settling with his beloved Wordsworths at Allan Bank in Grasmere.

Unfortunately his condition was such that even these old and once-admiring friends eventually grew tired of him. Wordsworth was reported as having called him a "rotten drunkard", and though he denied saying it, he may well have agreed with the sentiment. Coleridge left Allan Bank, and was to end by finding some stability, even contentment, not in Lakeland but in London, at the home of his doctor, James Gillman. There had been a time, however, when this unhappy man and brilliant poet had loved, and gained much from, the fells and the lakes, and it is good to remember him as he was when he wrote to Sara from the summit of Scafell.

Southey was to become Poet Laureate in 1813. In addition to being a poet he wrote histories and biographies, including the first book about Brazil (of which he was very proud, claiming that it would rival Gibbon's *Decline and Fall of the Roman Empire*) and a life of Nelson. The Lodore falls inspired him to an ingenious adjectival poem –

. .

And curling and whirling and purling and twirling,
And thumping and plumping and bumping and jumping,
And dashing and flashing and splashing and clashing,

. . .

and so on and so on.

Ironically, "The Three Bears", which he wrote for his children, is probably the only thing of his still known to the non-specialist – and even then, his authorship is not likely to be recognised, for in his version the porridge-stealer is an old woman, not Goldilocks. Today the visitor to Lakeland comes in search chiefly of Wordsworth, with a side-glance for Coleridge, and Southey is almost forgotten.

Keswick was also home to Peter Crosthwaite – "Admiral to the Keswick Regatta, Keeper of the Museum, Guide, Pilot, Geographer and Hydrographer to the Nobility and Gentry". Crosthwaite was an excellent self-publicist, but also a remarkable man. He did indeed make maps, at about three inches to the mile – and very accurate ones, too, although they had no contours marked. His regattas included boat races, of course, and also "sea battles": rowdy affairs with the hills "echoing to an amazing variety of sounds". His museum consisted of "many Hundred Natural and Artificial Curiosities, from every Quarter of the World" – fossils, plants, coins, birds, insects and so on. There were musical stones from the River Greta (!), two barnacles from the bottom of Captain Cook's boat and the stuffed result of a liaison between a Lakeland sheep and an escaped racoon – a lamb with claws not hooves, and wool in three colours. Crosthwaite noted in a 1792 advertisement that several "able Virtuosos" had declared, in 1784, that his museum was the best one north of the Trent. With the inclusion of many extra items it was now "improved as Three to One".

Keswick has always attracted eccentrics, it seems. In the mid-nineteenth century a Scot lived in a cave on Skiddaw, coming down to the town occasionally to get drunk and spend the night in jail. He was a phrenologist – and poet. One particularly fine verse of his is:

> A smell comes floating on the air,
> Although the fruitful source is hidden,
> I cannot see it anywhere,
> But think it is the village midden.

Anyone who wanted his bumps felt by a drunken poet who wrote stuff like that must, indeed, have needed his head examining.

To regain our starting-point, the car park at (266 196), a path that follows the eastern lake shore all the way from the boat houses south of the town can be followed. This path sees the best of the lake, with nearby islands and a backdrop of the Catbells ridge. The first island is Derwent Isle, horse-island to the Norse settlers. Beyond is Friar's Crag, named for the Lindisfarne monks who were ferried from here to the pilgrim isle of St Herbert. John Ruskin claimed that the view from Friar's Crag was one of the three loveliest in Europe, and his feeling for it is commemorated with a stone. Another stone is a memorial to Canon Rawnsley and, appropriately enough, the land around the Crag is owned by the National Trust. The Trust also owns The Ings, woodland on the shore of Strandshag Bay, where the walker is temporarily deflected from his water-line route. He returns to the water as Lord's Island is reached. This isle is owned by the Derwentwater family, lords (actually Earls) of the manor, and still holds the ruins of an early manor house. The house was destroyed in the Civil War when the family chose the Royalist side. In 1715 they were wrong again, opting for Stuart, a decision that cost the Earl his life. On the night before his execution an aurora, Derwent Water Lights, showed plainly in this place.

Distance

To Bassenthwaite Lake – 16km
and return

Derwent Water to Thirlmere

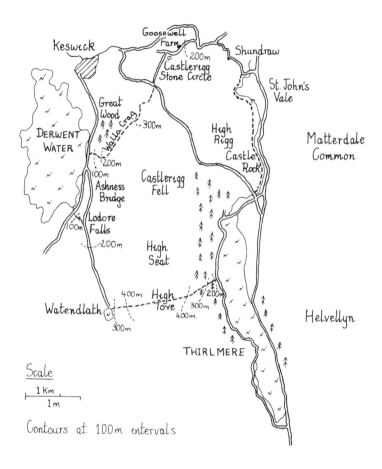

Keswick

Goosewell Farm

200m

Castlerigg Stone Circle

Shundraw

St. John's Vale

Great Wood

Walla Crag

300m

DERWENT WATER

200m

100m

Ashness Bridge

Castlerigg Fell

High Rigg

Castle Rock

Matterdale Common

Lodore Falls

100m

200m

High Seat

High Seat

Watendlath

400m

High Tove

200m

300m

400m

300m

Helvellyn

THIRLMERE

Scale

1 Km

1 m

Contours at 100m intervals

DERWENT WATER TO THIRLMERE

From the car park at (266 196) we must now reach Thirlmere, and the only real way is via Watendlath. To reach the hamlet there is a choice, with routes going south to Lodore falls, or slightly north to Ashness Bridge. Each of these is a permissive path, the only rights of way being further south, or via the minor road north of the Youth Hostel.

Lodore Falls is much photographed and admired, and in spate is a fine fall. It is reached by following the path beyond the wall gap just south (right) from the car park. The first fall to be heard, though pleasant, is not Lodore. Soon afterwards the sound of Lodore begins to help navigation towards it. Beyond the falls the pathways are distinct and easy to follow, keeping to the beck that feeds Lodore until a zig-zag path to the left is reached. This latter path leads to the Watendlath road.

When the road is reached the "Surprise View" of Derwent Water, and Ashness Bridge, are to the left, the way ahead is to the right. It may take a hard swallow to walk the round trip of two miles to see them, so thought should be given as to whether these two, rather than Lodore Falls, are to be visited. The bridge and view are reached directly through another gap in the wall just north of the car park, from which a distinct pathway leads to the top car park, beside the bridge. Ashness Bridge is even more frequently used to illustrate Lakeland than Lodore Falls, and is always well peopled. This popularity should not be allowed to detract from its beauty. It really is a splendid old pack-horse bridge, its elegance of line enhancing the delightful situation – set on water-washed rocks above a clear stream.

The view from "Surprise View" is equally fine, though the setting is more dramatic, a steep cliff and a sudden – and really quite surprising! – rift in the tree and valley rim that allows a view over Derwent Water to far Bassenthwaite Lake. The view is also the best place for seeing the Derwent Water floating island, should the visitor be lucky enough to be in Lakeland when one has surfaced.

From "Surprise View" to the top of the Lodore Falls zig-zag path the road is unfenced, and the walker can easily make his way through Ashness Wood, a beautiful piece of mainly broadleaf woodland.

Watendlath

Eventually the road is bounded, first on its western edge only, but eventually close-bounded, by walls that make the drive to Watendlath an unforgettable experience. Those wishing to visit the hamlet – and everyone should – can join Watendlath Beck in Ashness Wood and follow its western bank to the hamlet. Those anxious to reach Thirlmere can break out onto fell at any stage, heading for High Tove.

The Watendlath valley is an extraordinary place, the finest Lakeland example of the hanging valley, a glacial phenomenon caused by the overdeepening of a main valley – in this case Borrowdale. At any time the valley is worth visiting, but spring and autumn in Ashness woods show nature at her best. Summer can – if crowds permit – offer the tranquility of the beck and the steep rise of Caffel Side, and winter the sparkle of frost. Watendlath hamlet is a collection of cottages of finely textured stone beside a mirror tarn – a few good trees, a steep gill, a backdrop of high fell. Perfect Lakeland.

Ashness Bridge

The romantic name for this hidden hamlet cannot be precisely unscrambled. It is probable that it derives from a Norse name, together with *vatn* for lake, but could the valley have attracted earlier visitors? A pamphlet from the late 1920s suggests that the existence of gold in Borrowdale, and stone circles in the area, attracted the attention of the ancient Egyptians. So, many thousands of years ago, the Pharoah's people came, in search of wealth and famed spirituality. The second stone circle of Britain (after Stonehenge) was found just north of Embleton, at a site renamed for the Egyptian gods Set and Merti – Setmurthy. And in this hidden valley was a common highway – the *wa t ent reth*, the road of all men. Later they named *Sau-Re*, Sawrey, the children of Ra, the sun; and Wray itself. This is really rather appealing; the notions that can be dragged out from a few ill-understood words!

The way to Thirlmere from Watendlath is straightforward, following signs for Blea Tarn and Wythburn initially, but leaving that path as the fell wall turns away to go due east and upward for the summit of High Tove. The summit itself is visited, which at first sight is at variance with our preference for passes. But wait until the upper reaches of the fell are under your feet before passing judgement. Wainwright notes in his fell-guide that the summit is to be preferred because the depressions on either side are, firstly, little lower than the top and, secondly, water-logged even in the driest summer. As usual he is right, because the fell top is a bog for the last 400–500 feet.

High Tove has little to commend it – even the bogland seems sterile – but it is a direct and easily followed route to Thirlmere and, being arguably the centre of Lakeland, it has fine views in all directions, with almost all the main fell groups visible. A short walk along the ridge to High Seat allows Skiddaw, the only peak obscured from High Tove, to come into view.

Having viewed Helvellyn from High Tove, you might be surprised to learn that it is in the wrong place. It ought to be on our side of the valley: a clumsiness on the mountain's part which might never have been discerned had it not been for the wars which plagued mainland Europe at the end of the eighteenth century.

These wars prevented affluent Britishers from making the obligatory Grand Tour of Europe, leaving them with money to spend, time to kill and only their own island to travel in. An improving road and transport system simultaneously made journeys to the remoter parts of the island less difficult, so tourism within the country began – and was soon offering agreeable surprises. Britain was much more picturesque than its inhabitants had hitherto supposed . . . but you did have to go out and look for its picturesqueness. It was not long before this search had become a cult.

The name most closely associated with the cult of the Picturesque is that of William Gilpin, but he was not in fact its originator. It pre-dates by a good many years his famous book, published in 1786, and entitled *Observations relative chiefly to Picturesque Beauty, made in the year 1772, on several parts of England; particularly the Mountains and Lakes of Cumberland and Westmoreland.* The cult was embodied in guidebooks as a response to the tourists' need to be spared some of the tedious trundling necessary if they were to find the very best views. Guidebooks today have much the same purpose, but they do not have the same attitude.

This is largely because of the invention of photography. Modern tourists can take photographs or buy postcards, but if an eighteenth century tourist wanted to bring home a record of what he had seen, he must take out a pencil and sketch it. Views, therefore, came to be seen as the raw material for pictures even by people who were not going to portray them – and a surprisingly large number of people *did* make sketches very competently and quite as a matter of course. So the guide directed the tourist to the best view and then explained it in minute detail so that he could be sure it was perfect in balance and composition. In his guide to the River Wye (published in 1782, before his Lakeland book) Gilpin states: "Nature is always great in design. She is an admirable colourist also; and harmonizes tints with infinite variety and beauty; but she is seldom so correct in composition, as to produce an harmonious whole." He goes on to say that every view must comprise area, side-screens and front-screen, and that each of these may be simple or complex, and may contrast or fold. They can be adorned with ground, wood, rocks or buildings. The proportions and the colours must be correct. It must all be weighed up very carefully – a view might be ruined by a wrongly positioned tree.

The tourist for whom Gilpin wrote would be equipped with his Claude glass, a specially shaped mirror into which he peered so that he could see (over his shoulder!) the chosen view, reduced and framed. He could then sketch it. Gilpin would have told him, already, whether this particular view called for a pencil, or for water-colours.

William Gilpin, a clergyman born in 1724, near Carlisle, was the boldest of all the writers on the cult of the Picturesque, which he did so much to popularise. The rules he laid down were rigid, and he did not hesitate to take Nature to task. He it was who ordained that Helvellyn would look better on the other side of Thirlmere, because lakes improve mountains in the way that "an old head is greatly improved by the smoothness of the bald pate".

Gilpin is sublimely unaware of the subjectivity of his choice of "station", or view-point. He appears to believe that his rules are absolute, rather than matters of opinion, and this is particularly true when he is pronouncing on a very favourite subject: ruins. There are, he would have us know, two types of ruin, castles and abbeys, and "the most beautiful species of architecture in which our ruins are composed is called the Gothic". (Did you suppose that castles were originally "composed" for defence, abbeys for ecclesiastical purposes? Now you know better: they were built to be ruins.) In his book describing a journey down the River Wye by rowing boat, Gilpin goes so far as to suggest that the view would be improved if someone took a hammer to the ruins of Tintern Abbey: there is too much stone in their composition, and all of it is in the wrong place. Apparently he did not consider that Tintern Abbey would have been the better "for a group of banditti", as Dunmail Raise would have been. "Of all the scenes I ever saw this was the most adapted to the perpetration of some dreadful deed."

Not everyone approved of the cult of the Picturesque. In 1792 the one-armed Captain Joseph Budworth came, to walk 245 miles in a fortnight, to climb mountains that had almost certainly never before been climbed for "fun", and to tease the Lake Tourers. He sees them being rowed on a lake in their boat, and exclaiming: "God God! How delightful! How charming! I could live here for ever! Row on!"

From the summit head of High Tove, walk very slightly north of east to a wedge-shaped cleft in the conifers that surround Thirlmere, and follow the right (south) edge of the cleft downward to avoid the Cockrigg Crags. As the wedge narrows, the walker is funnelled to the correct exit onto the road that follows the western edge of the lake. There is no alternative to following this road left (northward) to the Thirlmere reservoir dam.

Many years ago this sheet of water was Wythburn Lake, or Leatheswater; though the name Thirlmere, from Thorolf's water for a Norse chieftain, or *thyrel mere* from its waisted shape, was used before it became a reservoir. It inspired Coleridge to talk of celebrating the world in its mirror, and of the surrounding crags with their covering of ferns and beech trees. It held on its shore Armboth, now only a name, but then a community with, at its heart, Armboth House that frightened everyone for miles with its supernatural visitors and ghostly banquets and its midnight lights. Then, in 1878, the Bishop of Manchester stood on Raven Crag and was enthralled. But not as Coleridge had been: the bishop's excitement was because he was sure that God had created Thirlmere with the express purpose of supplying water to Manchester. There was much dissent over the scheme, based on the interference with nature, the raising of the water level, and the unsafe nature of the aqueduct to transport the water – which might fail and drown many. But all to no avail. A dam was built, the water level was raised 50 feet, Armboth House was drowned – though no one cried for its loss – and Cottonopolis was supplied.

The dam was completed in 1890, built with the aid of a narrow-gauge railway that still excites the interested, and the reservoir was linked to Manchester by a 96-mile aqueduct that was a considerable engineering achievement. The apron of conifers was planted because it was believed that the trees generated, or attracted, clouds, though it was subsequently found that they drank far more water than they ever generated – if they generated any at all.

It is a century now since the reservoir was created, so what judgement can be passed on the scheme? The conifers are alien, but they do harbour red squirrels, for which a good deal of damage to the view can be tolerated. And the high cliffs of Raven Crag and beyond are still natural, a haven for trees that have learned to grow horizontally. But the lake edge has that unnatural tide mark born of abnormal water level changes, and the sterility that usually accompanies such lakes with their fences and anti-people notices. Not unnaturally the water authorities fear wholesale pollution of drinking supplies, but they do seem to exhibit an almost morbid fear of people. What do they think we will do in their water – that fish do not?

Besides Armboth House the rising waters covered two other spots that were associated with violent events. Sim's Cave was named from a man suspected of, but not convicted of, murder, who was ostracised by the dales folk and lived here fearing for his safety. And below the Helvellyn screes was Clark's Lowp, or Leap. A "Survey of the Lakes" from the late eighteenth century by James Clark tells the story of his namesake: "A man of the name of Clark was jealous of his wife to that degree that he was resolved to put an end to his own existence. He communicated his resolution to his wife, and told her at the same time, that he was determined to hang himself: to this she objected for fear that it might prove too painful: he then said he should shoot himself, but from this she likewise dissuaded him, for fear he might not kill himself outright, and so suffer extreme pain to no purpose: he next proposed to drown himself: this pleased her, and they went lovingly together to the water's edge: he then proposed to wade in, but she said the water was so cold, that he would suffer much needless pain; they then walked by the water-side till they came to this rock, which she told him she thought was fit for his purpose, as the water was deep enough at the edge to drown him; he was then going to throw himself directly in, but she told him he might hurt himself against the rock before he reached the water, so that he had better take a run and leap as far as he could: he followed her advice, very calmly put off his coat and took his leap; she staid till she saw him drowned, and then returned, fully satisfied that she had done her duty in giving him the best advice she could."

Perhaps the valley was cleansed of death and haunting by all the water.

To Return

From (315 195) take the footpath beside St John's Beck, and follow this through one of Lakeland's finest Vales, to the minor road at (309 230). Go across and take another path to Shundraw (308 236). Go left at the road and follow the road to Naddle Bridge (300 239). Now go west on a path to Goosewell Farm (295 238). Go left at the road and around to Castlerigg stone circle, one of Lakeland's best known archaeological sites, and the best placed of all. A minor road beside the circle is taken to the A591. Go straight across and take the path to (282 223). Go left to Rakefoot (284 221) and take the path above Walla Crag and Great Wood to Cat Gill (274 208). Follow the Gill down through the woods to Derwent Water.

Distances

Route from Derwent Water to Thirlmere – 10km
Return route –13km

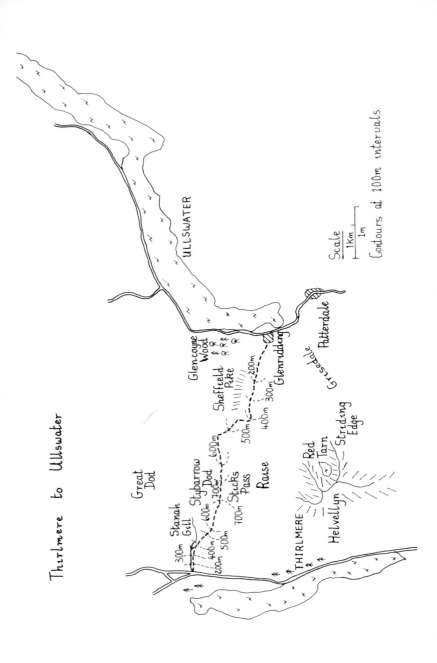

Thirlmere to Ullswater

ULLSWATER

Glen-coyne Wood

Great Dod

Stanah Gill
300m
200m
400m
500m

Stybarrow Dod
600m
700m
200m
Sticks Pass

Raise

Sheffield Pike
600m
500m
400m
300m
200m
Glenridding

Patterdale
Grisedale

THIRLMERE

Red Tarn
Helvellyn
Striding Edge

Scale
1Km
1m
Contours at 100m intervals

THIRLMERE TO ULLSWATER

From the Thirlmere dam the minor road is followed to the main Keswick to Ambleside road. The peace of Lakeland is indisputably broken here as cars speed along the newly widened and straightened road. It is to be hoped that the occupants do not miss the view to St John's Vale, one of the prettiest wide valleys in Lakeland, or the view of the Castle Rock of Triermain opposite where our route joins the main road.

Castle Rock was once called Green Crag but its name was changed when the legend of its transformation was printed – or should we say "invented"? – in the late eighteenth century. The story was that the rock was a castle of the fairy folk who transformed it into a crag if an inquisitive visitor came too close. From a distance, with a good deal of imagination, the crag could be termed castle-like. At a pinch.

The story of the fairy transformation of castle to crag to castle was used by Sir Walter Scott in the "Bridal of Triermain", an Arthurian fantasy in which the vanishing castle holds a sleeping princess sought by the Knight of Triermain. The Knight is the only person to have entered the castle, having succeeded in overcoming its magic to win his bride. Now the name Triermain is also linked to the Castle in the

Thirlmere from Sticks Pass

name of one of the most elegant rock climbs on the steep cliffs of the rock. South from Castle Rock, and actually leaving the minor road to Threlkeld rather than the main road, our route follows the well-signed route for Sticks Pass. Though well-signed the route is immediately ambiguous: bear left for the farm and go round it, thereafter follow, obviously, the track to Stannah Gill and beyond.

At 2420 feet the pass is the highest we shall cross, and in the initial stages where height is gained quickly it is steep, though never desperately so. The compensation is the view across Thirlmere to the south; to Skiddaw and Blencathra to the north and into Stannah Gill itself whose sheltered walls protect a tangled mass of fine trees and plants, beside a clear stream. When a ruined sheepfold is reached the worst is over. From there the pass launches itself at the grassy, gentle whale-backs that comprise the Helvellyn range. As far as the eye can see there are only grassy slopes, the edges of Helvellyn itself (on the eastern side above Red Tarn) being remarkable not only for their form, but for their existence at all in this prairie country. As if to confirm the gentleness of the country Helvellyn can claim to be the only 3000 foot peak in Britain on which an aircraft has landed. The idea of doing such a ridiculous thing belonged to Sir Sefton Brancker, who wished to alert the public to the possibilities of civil aviation. He wanted to use Snowdon, which was higher but turned out to be too sharp. Brancker inspected Helvellyn and declared it to be as smooth as a billiard table. And about the same size too, said pilot John Leeming when he climbed the hill to inspect his runway. A few rocks were moved and on December 15, 1926 Leeming with co-pilot Bert Hinkler, approached the hill in their two-seater, five cylinder, 100 HP engined Avro Gosport. Unfortunately it was raining and Leeming had to fly on, to land hurriedly with a rain-affected engine in a field near Windermere. Such was the novelty of flight that the local children poured out of the school convinced that Father Christmas had arrived. A week later the pair succeeded in landing, to the amazement of Professor E.R. Dobbs of Birmingham University who was on the top by chance. Dobbs witnessed a hastily written flight certificate and the plane took off again. The take-off run was very short, about thirty yards, so that it had to become airborne again by the expedient of flying off the edge of the hill, towards Red Tarn! Hinkler was finally to be killed when his plane flew into (another) mountain in low cloud.

The pass is named for a row of sticks that originally marked the route. These would have served as guides when the path was less eroded and as markers when a good snow covering obscured the trail. The gentle slopes can be deceptive: Helvellyn is far from gentle in adverse weather. There exist many graves of those who trifled with the hill, none more famous than that of a young Quaker named Gough, whose skeletal body was found many weeks after he had disappeared, still protected by his almost equally skeletal, but still alive, dog. Both Sir Walter Scott and Wordsworth eulogised the dog for its faithfulness.

Our route passes between the grassy humps of Stybarrow Dodd and Raise to bring into view the long comma of Ullswater. The path continues distinctly, passing, at a distance, a skiing hut, another reminder of the evenness of the terrain, and reaching old quarry workings and a reservoir. Here go right (south) and follow a zig-zag path down to the old Greenside mine. The mine was one of the oldest and largest lead mines in England, claimed to be 3000 feet at its deepest point. So important was the mine that it had electric lights installed in 1903. During its working life – and it was worked by the Romans – it yielded one million tons of ore which gave 100,000 tons of concentrate with 79 per cent lead content and ten ounces of silver to the ton. It also produced spoil heaps and left rusting ruins. Yet

Sticks Pass

Ullswater

these seem less incongruous than the odd plastic wrapper and ring-pull can.

Beyond the mine – the route is signed through the maze of buildings – the path leads towards Glenridding Beck to find the old mine road. To the left (north) the Glenridding screes on the side of Sheffield Pike form another waste tip. At the bottom of the Greenside road is Glenridding, whose church has a chalice of local silver, and Ullswater.

Ullswater is, probably, Ulf's lake. Ulf and Thorof, if the latter is the origin of Thirlmere, were enviable Norsemen, holding two of the finest valleys in Lakeland. Ullswater is the second largest lake, a couple of miles shorter than Windermere and about as deep. The difference in geology means that Ullswater is more rugged, its backdrops more uncompromising, except at the extreme northern tip where it softens. By Pooley Bridge it is almost civilised. By then it is only four miles from the M6.

On Ullswater, in July 1955, Donald Campbell drove *Bluebird* through the 200 mph barrier. Only later did he transfer his attempts to Coniston.

As with Windermere the lake, despite its size, froze in the great winters of earlier centuries. "In the yeare of our Lord 1607 . . . was a marvellous grete frost which continued from the 1st daie of December until the 16th daie of Februarie after. Ullswater was frozen over . . . so strong that men in grete companies mad a common way (upon it)." There was dancing and, on Shrove Tuesday, a bonfire and skating. In 1883 a man arrived at Pooley Bridge one night after a ride over "the biggest field in my life". He had ridden over the snow-covered lake.

Also like Windermere, the lake has a steamer plying between several landing stages. In older days the steamers had several guns on deck that were fired to arouse the wonderful echoes from the shore cliffs in the southern reaches. It is claimed that on one occasion twenty-five reverberations were counted. Another gun, shore-mounted near Patterdale, habitually produced six or seven echoes. Todays tourists prefer the scenic beauty of the lake shores to echoes. Most visit Aira Force, perhaps the best of Lakeland falls, and certainly the one most steeped in legend. Wordsworth set "The Somnambulist" there, another Arthurian fantasy with a wonderful title. The sleepwalker in question is a baron's daughter who awaits the return of her beloved, Sir Eglamore, an Arthurian knight away fighting evil. Her doubts about his love cause her to sleepwalk and on

Ullswater

the night of his return she walks towards him. He touches her and in her fear she leaps away to fall over the force. Despite Sir Eglamore's efforts she drowns and he, grief stricken, becomes a recluse further up the Aira Beck glen. Our route does not visit Aira Force, going south from Glenridding to round the southern tip of the lake at Patterdale.

Patterdale is Patrick's Dale, for the lake valley was said to have been visited by St Patrick. He baptised the dale folk from a local well – St Patrick's well – that we have passed. At a later time the village was on the route for marauding Scots moving south, to such an extent that the local men practised archery regularly. No one was excused and everyone had to work at it "until they could hit a Scot at twenty-five yards". A fairly precise way of measuring expertise.

The strife brought by the Scots may explain the existence of Kings of Patterdale, hereditary title-holders from the Mounsey family. It is believed that the first such king led a force that rebuffed a raiding party. This was probably in the early seventeenth century, with the line lasting for about 150 years. The Mounsey kings lived in a house called, of course, the Palace, though the last one, a tight-fisted individual, left it in favour of claiming free meals – to which he maintained he was entitled – from his subjects. He dressed in rags and repeatedly hid his money in holes in walls. After his death his son failed to find any cash that did exist and, in disgust, sold up and left. If the visitor has an hour to kill in Patterdale he could do worse than probe the odd wall section or two.

Such dishonourable behaviour was not limited to the Patterdale royalty. A Cumberland and Westmoreland wrestling champion once lost his title to a Patterdale man in a best-of-three contest. Only later was it discovered that the Patterdale man was twins who swapped kit between the fights.

To Return

There is no reasonable return route that does not involve high fell walking, other than to reverse the outward route.

Distance

Route from Thirlmere to Ullswater –8km

Ullswater
to
Haweswater

ULLSWATER

Howtown

Hallin
Fell

200 m

Martindale
Church   Fusedale

300 m

High
Dodd

400 m

500 m

300 m

Silver
Crag

Boardale

Martindale

Wether
Hill

Place
Fell

Beda
Fell

600 m   500 m

400 m

300 m

Patterdale

High
Kop

Measand
Beck

Red
Crag

HAWESWATER

High
Raise

High
Street

Riggindale
Crag

Blea
Tarn

Mardale Head

Scale

1 Km

1 m

Contours at 100 m intervals

ULLSWATER TO HAWESWATER

In Patterdale a footpath is signed for Howtown (and Boredale) next to the "George Starkey Hut", and at Side Farm the left (north-west) branch is taken for the southern tip of Ullswater. From here to Sandwick, or even on to Howtown, is one of the finest lakeside walks in Lakeland. There is birch here, and juniper and larch – even a turkey oak at one point. The crags that fall off of Place Fell are an endless rock garden, and the lake views are superb, across to Glencoyne Wood and the sculpted side of the Helvellyn range. In autumn this area is particularly good, the trees splendid in their golds and reds. In winter there is solitude; a fine drizzle ripples the lake as a little grebe dives for breakfast.

The lake-shore path is easily followed, winding inland and upward for even better views before reaching the hamlet of Sandwick (423 197). Go right (south) here until a path for Howtown is signed at Bridge End (426 194). We are not going to Howtown, but follow the path to Hallin Bank and down to the bridge over Sandwick Beck (434 190). This is a delightful spot. The wide beck has produced small water-meadow strips on each side; the bridge itself is excellent – perhaps best described as second generation clapper; and finally there is the view to Martindale, with the high peaks of High Street beyond.

Martindale is named from the church of St Martin which surprises the newcomer with its isolated presence. The first church here, dedicated to St Martin of Tours, was constructed in the thirteenth century. Traces of this original church still protrude from the south wall of the present building, which dates from 1633. The little church is delightful with its lengthwise pews and tiny windows.

The first vicar of the new church, Richard Birkett, was another of the army of thrifty Lakeland pastors. He founded a school in the dale the fees of which were two weeks free board and lodging in the parental home, and eggs in other weeks which were checked for size against a hole in a wooden board. All his pay was saved and loaned at 10 per cent per annum. He kept a cow in the churchyard – though he did clean cowpats off the graves – and so objected to molehills that he caught and killed the moles with his bare hands. When he was

eighty-one years old he married a lady with the good dowry of £60, only to die shortly after, leaving her a fortune of £1,300.

The church later owned a corn mill on the dale's Howegrain Beck, though clearly this was a less than lucrative and easily managed asset. The church steward at one stage felt compelled to write to the miller, a letter that administers a considerable kick on the shins at first, becoming a model of politeness at the end: "If you do not immediately take care to repair the mill in such parts as you ought, I shall be obliged to take such course to compel you as will not be very grateful to you. I am your friend . . ."

The route forward is straightforward enough, following the path alongside the churchyard wall. The route is easily followed, though occasionally, and especially near the top, the path is indistinct. At Brownthwaite Crag (443 173) the view back down into Martindale is excellent. The path is heading for Keasgill Head (453 169) a low point, though hardly a pass, on the High Street Roman road ridge. High Street, though appearing to contradict the Roman edict of minimum effort in moving men from one point to another, was a marvellous piece of military planning. The ridge here is straight, and high enough both to prevent ambush, and to allow policing of the important Ullswater valley that led, via Kirkstone Pass, to the Galava fort at Ambleside. In the right conditions – a misty day and the wind echoing around the fell tops – you can convince yourself that the rhythmic noise is the feet of legionaries and soon, from the gloom will appear a ghostly, shimmering army of Romans.

From Keasgill Head the uncharted ground of High Kop is crossed, with a short descent to pick up a path that has crossed Wether Hill and is heading gently downward towards Low Kop, plucking up the courage to throw itself down the steep valley side of Measand Beck to reach first the Beck and then Haweswater.

Haweswater is the only other lake apart from Thirlmere that is wholly a reservoir. Though Ennerdale, Ullswater and Windermere are used as water sources, only Haweswater and Thirlmere were enlarged to act as storage tanks and provide water in such bulk that their edges have that particular reservoir bath-ring. Haweswater also provides for thirsty Manchester, though its usage did not start until 1940. At 18,400 million gallons it has twice Thirlmere's capacity. The dam, at the northern end, is a huge structure, built, in part, with stone from Mardale church and thoughtfully tree-clad.

Haweswater

Our route follows Measand Beck into the reservoir. The beck falls through Fordingdale, a delightful enclosed valley with a series of waterfalls at the lower end that are especially conspicuous from the far side of Haweswater. This is due less to their height and volume – though that too is impressive – than to their position, exposed rather than tucked away in a deep gill. Measand was a hamlet drowned by the rising waters. It is not the name Measand that is remembered, however, but Mardale from the southern end of the lake.

In the long drought of 1984 the village of Mardale was returned to the valley. The houses had been bulldozed, but stone walls remained and the old arched bridge still crossed Mardale Beck. When Haweswater was two miles long Mardale was beautifully set at its head; in 1984 it was necessary to trek in across the cracked mud herding perhaps – as I did, however inadvertently – a flock of Canada geese, to wonder at the water-bleached stones. Now lichen-free, the low walls really did look like the skeleton of a lost community.

On some weekends in that hot summer there were more people in Mardale than could ever have been there before the village disappeared. They talked in whispers of where the Dun Bull pub had been, of the strangeness of it all. It was as though they were standing in a graveyard. And in a sense we were, for when Mardale drowned, the valley died. There used to be horse racing on High Street, at 2500 feet, with beer carted up by the barrel. The parties that followed shepherd's and huntsmen's meets lasted for days. No more. That was the price paid for the water.

Until 1729 Mardale had no hallowed ground, and bodies were taken along the Corpse Road, still marked on the Ordnance Survey maps, to Shap. In 1736 John Holme was the last dalesman to be taken

Mardale, 1984

on that journey. When the water was coming relatives of those who lay in the Mardale cemetary were offered the chance of re-interment. Few took up the offer.

John Holme was in the line of an early dalesman, Hugh Holme, a southerner who fled here in 1208 to escape the vengeance of King John after an abortive plot against him. He hid in Hugh's cave, still there below Riggindale, outlived the king and stayed.

In another drought, take the chance to visit Mardale. If instead you come in normal circumstances, the Dun Bull is under fifteen feet of water and the valley is silent. The walk along the shore from Measand to Mardale Head (469 108) is awkward in places, but the views ahead to Riggindale and Harter Fell are particularly fine. The wooded promontary of The Rigg, and Wood Howe are elegant, and the chaffinches at the Head car park will eat biscuits from your hand. It is a fine place, Mardale.

But it is sad that to achieve immortality as a village it is necessary to drown.

To Return

Without doubt the finest way to return to Patterdale is by lake steamer from Howtown, reached by regaining High Street and descending via Fusedale directly into Howtown.

Distances

Route from Ullswater to Haweswater –16km
Route along Haweswater to Mardale Head –7km
Return from Haweswater to Howtown –8km

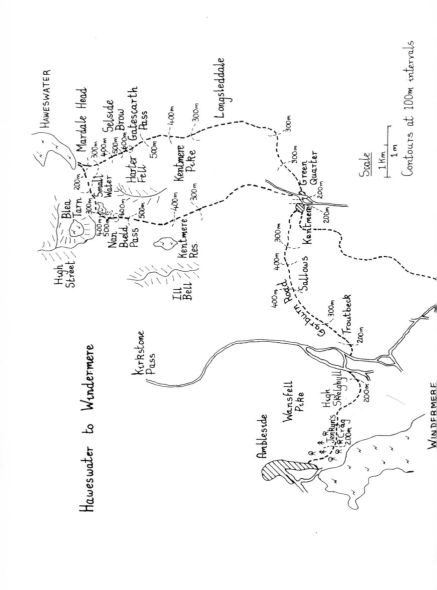

Haweswater to Windermere

HAWESWATER

Mardale Head

Selside
Goat Scar
Brow
Gatescarth Pass

Longsleddale

High Street

Blea Tarn

Small Water

Nan Bield Pass

Harter Fell

Kentmere Pike

200m
300m
400m
500m
400m
500m
300m
400m
500m
400m
600m
300m
400m
500m
300m

Ill Bell

Kentmere Res.

Green Quarter

Kentmere

200m
300m
200m
200m

Kirkstone Pass

Wansfell Pike

Garburn Road

Sallows

Troutbeck

400m
400m
300m
300m
200m

Ambleside

High Skelghyll

Jenkyn's Crag

200m

200m

WINDERMERE

Scale
1 Km
1 m
Contours at 100m intervals

HAWESWATER TO WINDERMERE

Those who do not wish to visit the car park at Mardale Head can head straight up towards the Nan Bield Pass from the footbridge over Mardale Beck (467 108). From the car park a Manchester Water Works signpost points the way. The path to the Pass is easy to follow up into the secluded hollow filled by Small Water. All Lakeland travellers have their favourite spots – here is mine. Once in this place I heard croaking in stereo, as the call of a passing member of the crow family was answered by an amorous toad in the lake shallows. The view towards Haweswater is tremendous, and yet the whole of Mardale can be excluded by just walking back from the Small Water *cwm* rise, if the Celtic word for such a hollow may be permitted. The Crag at the back of the hollow is imposing, but a path up it does exist, threading its steep but straightforward way after passing, near the lake, some odd rock shelters. Presumably these would have been for shepherds and dogs.

Perhaps also they were used by huntsmen, for here, as everywhere, there is a tradition of hunting. During one such hunt in 1787 a man named Dixon fell from above Blea Water Crag, above the lake a little north of Small Water, in the next hollow of this beautifully sculpted side of High Street. Dixon fell 1000 feet, bashing his head so often that he was scalped. He stood up and hollered up the crag that the fox had gone out of the end of the hollow and that if the dogs were loosed he would follow on soon. He then collapsed, but made a full recovery, having suffered only bruising. They were a tough breed that worked those hills for a livelihood.

Nan Bield is a high pass, a rock doorway to the Kentmere valley which opens up to the south. The descent into it is straightforward, following the path to Overend (464 057) where the higher, grassy track is followed to reach a green lane that leads to the Kentmere road at (462 044). The road is followed to the village.

There is little to the village, though St Cuthbert's church has a memorial to one very famous son. Bernard Gilpin was born here in 1517, and was brought up at the Hall. Once, when he was five, a group of visiting friars were entertained and following a convivial evening one preached on the Sunday, holding forth on the evils of the

demon drink. Young Bernard pointed out loudly, in that delightful way that young children have, that this man who spoke against drunkenness had himself been drunk the night before, and his mother "made speed to stop the child's mouth with her hand that he might speak no more".

Gilpin went to Oxford when he was sixteen and was ordained in 1541. At first he was a staunch Catholic, but later turned Protestant. In practice he was neither, caring nothing for the battle between Latin and English, wanting only to worship his God and to work for social justice. When Queen Mary came to the throne he feared for his life, asking his wife to have prepared at all times a clean gown for his execution. But though he was arrested the Queen died and he was released. Thereafter he toured the north of England preaching and easing the burden of the poor. Such was his fame that a thief who stole his horse returned it when he discovered that it belonged to the "Apostle of the North". He was, however, held to be, in part at least, responsible for the northern Catholic rebellion in 1569, further proof of his ambivalent relationship to the question of protestantism. He died in 1583, "his lean body quite worne out with diversity of paines-taking".

Kentmere Hall

Kentmere Hall, where Gilpin was raised, lies a little to the east of the hamlet itself. It is not visited by our route, though seen from it, but the detour is minimal. There, also, are the remains of a pele tower from the fourteenth century. As mentioned in the Historical Introduction, such fortifications were common at the edges of Lakeland, but very unusual in so remote a spot.

Our route follows the Garburn Road from Kentmere. Some experts believe this name derives from "muddy stream". Burn for stream? There are many stories of Scots invading this north-east corner of Lakeland: one has them following the Mardale, Nan Bield, Kentmere route and being ambushed and killed here. Were incursions so frequent that the Scots named their invasion route, and the inhabitants of Kentmere needed a pele tower to protect them?

The route to the Garburn Pass, the last pass on our journey around Lakeland – we are moving back onto the hub of the spoked wheel of lakes – is signed as we leave the hamlet (454 044). At first the path is on open fell, but when the pass itself is reached an enclosed road, the Garburn Road, is followed. Go right where Dubbs Road leaves off south (421 032) and on to The Howe, and the main road at (412 026). At this junction of roads ancient and modern, Garburn Road is not signed, but is obvious enough as the first track to the left after leaving Trout Beck.

The ancient road we have followed, contouring down around the flank of Sour Howes, has a distinctly unmetalled appearance. In 1730 a survey of Lakeland roads by the High Constable of Kendal noted that they were all bad but that Garburn was "soe much out of repair and in decay, that a great part of it is not passable for either man or horse to travel through the said ways without danger of being bogged in moss or lamed among the stones". Despite the enclosing walls, erosion by the fell becks has continued, and what we follow is probably much like the road the High Constable complained of two and a half centuries ago.

If the road was old enough local legend would doubtless blame its state on Hugh Hird, a local giant who was undoubtedly real and very strong even if he was not as tall as some of the stories told of him and his height. Hugh gained a local reputation for some remarkable feats, including picking up a thirty-foot oak beam during construction of Kentmere Hall, and once routing a band of marauding Scots apparently by throwing trees at them. He was a quiet lad who lived with his mother in a tied cottage in Troutbeck. The estate agent attempted to evict the pair, an action which, luckily for the agent, did not provoke Hugh's wrath, but sent him off to London to plead his

The Garburn road

mother's case before Edward IV. He agreed to wrestle the King's champion but when he threw the man the partisan crowd shouted foul. Incensed, Hugh picked the champion up bodily and, so the story goes, broke his back, threw him off the stage and asked if that constituted a sufficiently fair and decisive throw. It seems unlikely that he really broke the man's back, rather that the term was used to signify a total mastery. Impressed, the King pronounced Hugh champion, and gave the cottage to his mother. Hugh returned home, dying in Troutbeck after injuring himself pulling trees up by the roots.

At the base of the Garburn Road our route enters the Troutbeck valley followed by the Roman road before the march up to the ridge of High Street. Go right at the main road (413 026), and, after crossing Trout Beck by Church Bridge, go left up to one corner of the widely, but sparsely, spread village of Troutbeck.

The countryside here is pastoral again. We have crossed the band of Coniston limestone and are back in farmland – the grass so good that cows fed on it produce milk so creamy that "a mouse might walk over it dryshod".

Beside the Post Office (406 026) signs tell us that the lane will lead

Jenkyn's Crag, Windermere

on to Skelghyll Wood, Jenkyn's Crag and Ambleside. The lane skirts open fell to enter the wood, another of Lakeland's fine pieces of woodland. At Jenkyn's Crag Windermere, which has been glimpsed before, is suddenly revealed as the huge sheet of water it is. The crag is steep and has unimpaired views down to the lake and its western shore. On a clear day, when the angular peaks of Langdale form a backdrop to northern Windermere, there are few better views on our journey.

From the Crag the route continues easily through the wood until the delightfully named Stencher Beck is reached. Here the walker who wants to visit the National Trust's Stagshaw Gardens takes the path that follows the beck downwards (south-west). Those heading for Ambleside continue to descend north of west to the road at (377 032) if they are looking for the Galava site, or at (377 037) if they are looking for the main town.

Because of the Roman association many have tried to find a Latin origin for the town's name. One suggestion is that it derives from *amabilis*, loveable, because it was a *situs amabilis*, a loveable sight to the hard-pressed legionaries returning from a few weeks at Hard

Knott, or a march across High Street. This has a certain romantic appeal, but the more logical explanation is a Norse name, derived from "dairy pasture" and "water", indicative of Ambleside's position and the lushness of the local grassland.

Quite why Ambleside should have become the important centre during the medieval development of Lakeland is not obvious. Clearly its position was important. Indeed it may have been crucial, because a local cloth industry developed despite the absence of a fulling mill. The town had a wool market and two fairs by the mid-seventeenth century, having won the local battle for supremacy over Grasmere and Rydal. Later there was a bobbin mill, this explaining the fine stocks of oak and hazel in the area. Ash grows here, too, its leaves having been used for winter cattle food. This use of the leaves for food was very important – the pastorage was excellent, but the Lakeland climate has always hindered the farmer. In the seventeenth century a local bye-law decreed that "whosoever doth cutt down or breake any other Men's Ash Leaves forfeits 1 shilling".

Such snippets shed a little light on the way of life of long-gone Lakelanders. Another interesting sidelight is that school festivals in the last quarter of the seventeenth century included cock-fighting, with the children given cock-pennies for betting on the birds. One child who attended such festivals later became Bishop of Carlisle.

One hundred years after those school festivals Ambleside had fallen upon hard times. The houses were falling down, the inhabitants poverty-stricken. The market had not survived the decline of the wool industry and had become a local joke. It was said that the Ambleside market started at twelve, but finished at noon; and that if you saw a man with a lantern in the streets you knew he was looking for the market.

Somehow the town survived, and with the coming of tourism it began to flourish again. A guide published in 1891 extolled the virtues of the town as a health resort.

The reason was ozone. The Rev. Thomas Mackereth FRAS, FR Met. Soc. and Meterological Observer for Westmoreland, had measured Ambleside's ozone as 6 – though 6 what is not too clear – in comparison to the 0 of Manchester, Liverpool etc. This was excellent, for it is the best of best antiseptics. And, adds the guide, the town *has a sewage works!*

Today the town is still an excellent tourist centre. Its lakeside is less obtrusive than Bowness, its centre is less obviously given over to the tourist industry, maintaining some independence, some touch of its past. A walk through the town is worthwhile, if only to see Bridge House, which must be the National Trust's oddest possession.

Ambleside

One early arrival in the wave of writers and live-in tourists who made their way to the Ambleside area in the mid-nineteenth century was Harriet Martineau. Born in 1802 in Norwich, she arrived here in 1846 already established as a radical writer and reformer. She supported the French revolutionaries and the American negro slaves, and was an early campaigner for women's rights. At her house, The Knoll, she dug a hole in the garden and bathed nude in it when it was filled with rainwater. She was visited by Charlotte Brontë and George Elliot, and was a friend of the Wordsworths, though all these friendships were made difficult by her deafness. She eventually declined evening invitations to Wordsworth's house because a conversation between herself and the poet was virtually impossible once he had taken out his teeth and started to mumble into her ear trumpet. It is not pleasant to make sport from other people's disabilities but the picture conjured up of the pair of them is undeniably funny.

But though deaf, Miss Martineau was a fine speaker on a wide range of social topics. At one lecture in Ambleside on the perils of alcoholism her arguments, backed with drawings of drink-affected insides, were so strong that one well-known local drunk had to go outside to be sick.

Ms Martineau died in Ambleside in 1876. Seventy years later another original thinker arrived in the town, the German artist and writer Kurt Schwitters. By that time Schwitters was almost sixty, and was seeking peace for the last years of his life. Driven by Hitler into fleeing Germany in 1937 he had settled in Norway only to find it invaded by the very people from whom he had fled. He escaped to London, but was interned as an alien. Schwitters had a new approach to art – Merz, a total concept with writing, recitation, painting and sculpture. He abandoned representational forms and even, finally, the accepted media. At Elterwater, in the old gunpowder store, he created a Merzbau, a barn as art with shaped walls in plaster and stone. It can still be seen at Newcastle University.

He did not enjoy the peace of Ambleside for long. In the January of 1948 Schwitters died, in Kendal. There are those who still remember him, an odd man making a living by painting with bus tickets.

To Return

Retrace the main route above Jenkyn's Crag back to Troutbeck Post Office (408 027). Go right along the road to (408 020) and there take the path east to the main road at (411 019). Go right and right again at (411 018). Follow the road to (435 996) where a footpath goes north to Kentmere. From Green Quarter (461 041) take the path northeast to Longsleddale and follow the River Sprint back up towards the Gatescarth Pass. Go over the Pass and down to Mardale Head.

This section can be split at Kentmere.

Distances

Route from Haweswater (Mardale Head) to Kentmere −9km
   from Kentmere to Windermere (Ambleside) −11$^{1}/_{2}$km
Return route, Ambleside to Kentmere −16km
   Kentmere to Mardale Head −9km

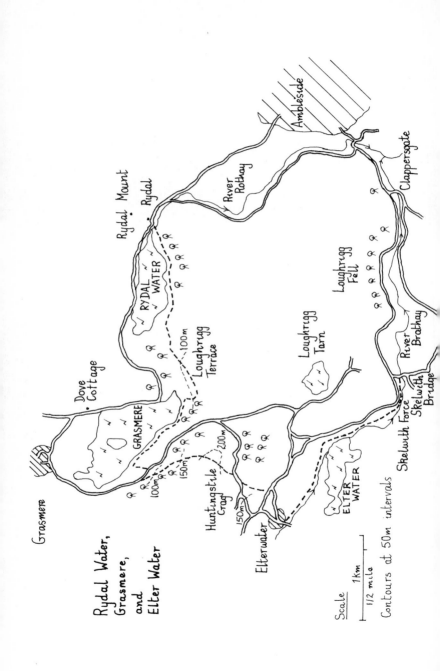

Grasmere

Rydal Water,
Grasmere,
and
Elter Water

Dove
Cottage

GRASMERE

Rydal Mount
Rydal

RYDAL
WATER

River
Rothay

Ambleside

Clappersgate

Loughrigg Terrace

100m

Loughrigg Fell

Huntingstile Crag

200m

150m

100m

150m

Loughrigg Tarn

River Brathay

Skelwith Force
Skelwith Bridge

Elterwater

ELTER
WATER

Scale
1km
1/2 mile

Contours at 50m intervals

RYDAL WATER, GRASMERE AND ELTERWATER

Our route leaves Ambleside by the path heading westward beside the church whose form is indicative of the town's earliest prosperity. The path crosses the River Rothay to emerge on the minor road at (371 045). Turn right.

The route follows this road with the river dominating the view right, and the wooded flank of Loughrigg fell crowding in from the left. Set below the woodland are a row of elegant houses. Fox Howe, the exception to the right of the road, was owned once by Dr Arnold of Rugby school fame, and later lived in by his son Matthew. Loughrigg Holme was owned by Edward Quillinan whose second wife was Dora Wordsworth, beloved daughter of William. The other side of the Rothay from the house, in a field beside the A591 are the

The River Rothay, near Ambleside

remains of the old Rydal Hall. Though often said to have been abandoned during construction the old hall was both finished and occupied. But there were always problems with the site, probably even during the building. Three headless ghosts – as if one was not enough! – danced there, and a spectral white dog was seen. At night there were "lamentations" that wore down the occupiers and the neighbours. Eventually the spirits won and the hall was abandoned. A new hall was built, on Rydal Beck were the village is now situated, using stone from the original site. As always there were legends about the old hall, but ultimately the neighbours were more concerned with treasure said to be buried there, or in an underground passage said to lead between the old and new sites. Behind the new hall are Rydal falls, a delightful spot. Once a guide was needed to visit the falls – there was no admittance without one. Today it is free, but appreciation can be shown by "transferring a small coin". Our route leads to the A591 and left into Rydal.

At Rydal Mount William Wordsworth spent the last thirty-seven years of his life, dying there on 23 April 1850, at eighty years of age, from pleurisy. 23 April is St. George's Day, and also the day on which Shakespeare died.

Since Rydal Mount was the house in which Wordsworth spent the longest period of his life, and was where he died, and in Rydal village, behind the church, is Dora's Field with its spring-time daffodils, it would be easy to assume that it would also be the centre of the industry that has grown up around the poet. Not so – it is Dove Cottage and Grasmere that receive the lion's share of attention and it is when our route reaches them that we shall consider in more detail the most famous Lakelander of them all. But do visit Rydal Mount. There Wordsworth the gardener created the still attractive garden. It is a more intimate spot than crowd-thronged Dove Cottage.

Our route leaves Rydal along the A591 taking a hole in the wall to the left of the road, opposite the Glen Rothay Hotel. Going through this hole is like stepping through Alice's looking glass. Behind is high speed metal, all noise and rush. In front is a short path to a small bridge over the Rothay and green meadow to Rydal Water, all peace and timelessness. This short section of our route is as good as any on the journey, and encapsulates its purpose – water seen against fell.

Rydal Water was once *Routha mere*, the lake of the river that is now the Rothay. The name derives from "trout stream", confirming the story that the Windermere char migrate up-Brathay, while the trout go up-Rothay. The new name Rydal could be a mispronunciation born of ages, but seems hardly likely to have affected lake and not river. More likely it is from the dale of the rye, since this was a highly fertile valley, and is known to have grown cereals in the past. But irrespective of the name this lake, viewed through a framework of fine trees, set with tree-topped islands, is exquisite. It is easy to see why a generation of poets could find voice to their feelings in these surroundings. How can Nathaniel Hawthorne, the American writer, have felt that this is just "a flood in a field"?

Our route moves easily along the southern edge of the flooded field to reach, at (348 060), a path emerging from the woodland that has risen from the western tip of Rydal Water. This western tip – there is a car park here – is a fine piece of wetland with bog plants, insects and birds. Paths lead to the water's edge where the visitor stands on what feels disconcertingly like a floating vegetation path. The other side of the A591 from here is White Moss Common where Wordsworth skated on the pond, and where he caught the pleurisy that killed him. Below it a minor road links the A591 with Dove Cottage and Grasmere.

William Wordsworth was born in Cockermouth, on the north-western fringe of Lakeland on 7 April 1770, the second of five children to a lawyer father and a mother who came from, they decided, one of the better families in Penrith, on the north-eastern fringe of Lakeland. Third born of the five children was Dorothy, the only girl, whose sisterly devotion was to be both protection and inspiration to William in later life.

Wordsworth's birthplace is open to the public, and is still the best house in Cockermouth. Its splendour was not matched by the family's wealth. William's father was steward to the Lowther family – one of north England's richest families – and appears never to have been paid for his work. After his father's death William and his brother fought a long and difficult court case claiming a fortune in unpaid salary. The case was won, but Lowther refused to pay, a refusal that he took to the grave. Eventually the money was paid, but by then William had endured a hand-to-mouth adolescence, and was not best pleased with the English aristocracy.

When time came for his schooling William at first went to the local Cockermouth school, along with Fletcher Christian later to achieve

Rydal Water

notoriety on the *Bounty*. Later he transferred to a school in Penrith where he was at odds with his mother's relatives. They appear to have been pretentious and young William, a junior hippy, saw them as snobs. They saw him as in need of discipline and were probably glad to get rid of him to Hawkshead school in 1779, where he was sent with his brothers following the death of his mother. Dorothy was sent away to relatives in Yorkshire and her separation from William caused her great pain.

At Hawkshead the boys stayed with Ann Tyson, a local widow, who treated them very kindly. William used his free time to explore the local countryside, developing a love for natural things and a passion for skating. He stayed with Ann Tyson for eight years, until he went to St John's College, Cambridge. Half way through this eight year period Wordsworth's father died, and it was left to his uncles to support him at college. They were not enthralled with his behaviour, which was very anti-establishment, despite his later efforts to portray

Rydal Water

himself as studious. In his rebelliousness he was not unusual, even for his time, but his 1790 walkabout in Europe was ahead of its time, and not without danger. He visited Italy and Switzerland, but to do so had to travel through France at a time when the Revolution was in full swing.

The following year, having obtained an indifferent degree and not knowing what to do next he returned to France. There, in Orleans, he had a passionate affair with Annette Vallon, a girl a few years older than himself who became pregnant and gave birth to a daughter Caroline, after Wordsworth had returned to England. The affair, and the existence of Caroline, only became common knowledge after Wordsworth's death, and was not in keeping with his later character. His desertion of his lover was not as bad as it seems. War had recently been declared and there were much less dangerous places for an Englishman than France. The war went on for twenty years, effectively preventing Wordsworth from returning to marry Annette, as, apparently, had been his intention in the earliest days.

Back in England William suffered badly, presumably as a result of leaving Annette and the child back in France. He failed as a political journalist in London and left, with Dorothy, for two years in Dorset and Somerset. Dorothy had re-entered his life as his devoted companion and as true believer in his talent. She also appears to have kept him sane during the severe, almost suicidal, depression that followed. Dorothy was aware of what had happened, accepted it and wrote to Annette in a friendly way. Another who helped was Samuel Taylor Coleridge whom they met in Dorset. He and William were instantly fascinated with each other and drove each other on to dizzy heights as they explored their talents. Coleridge lived, at that time, in Somerset and the Wordsworths followed him there. The three, not the best dressed people in the area by far, went on long walks loudly reciting poetry. They walked at night, they carried a telescope and, eventually, they were investigated by the Home Office because the locals thought they were French spies!

The friendship with Coleridge resulted in *Lyrical Ballads* in 1798, most of the work in which was William's. It was published anonymously, but they were both paid rather well. Wordsworth was now, it seems recovered and after a trip to Germany he returned to the Lake District. This time it was for good.

William and Dorothy found a house in Grasmere. It had no name, but at one time had been an inn, the Dove and Olive Branch, so they called it Dove Cottage. The peace allusion suited both of them. High above it the lion and lamb rocks of Helm Crag nodded an assurance that their new valley was a place of peace.

Many visitors believe that Dove Cottage was William's only home, though in fact he lived there for only nine of his fifty-one Lakeland years. But with Dorothy's inspiration the time at Dove Cottage was William's most productive period. Only recently has Dorothy's own journal been taken seriously in its own right, rather than analysed for its influence on William, for its thoughts on William, even for indications of an incestuous relationship with William. The journal reveals a deep love of nature, and a wonderful talent for expressing that love. It was Dorothy who saw the daffodils and pointed them out to William's lonely cloud.

When Coleridge moved to Greta Hall, Keswick, the situation was perfect for the flowering of talent. Now it was Lakeland locals the three frightened with their clothes, odd hours and recitations. But the idyll was not to last. William married Mary Hutchinson, who doted on him as unselfishly as his sister did, and although Dorothy – in spite of initial heartbreak – remained close to them both her inspirational influence was probably reduced; and Coleridge became increasingly unhappy at Keswick.

William and Mary had their first child, John, in 1803, adding four more by 1810, though two died in childhood. The extra family made a move from Dove Cottage imperative and they took Allan Bank and the Parsonage, both in Grasmere for a couple of years each before moving into Rydal Mount in 1813. Thomas De Quincey had now arrived in Grasmere, a hero-worshipping boy come in search of the subject of his adoration, and preparing to tell the world about the Lake Poets. He never lost his respect for Wordsworth's talent, though he lost his friendship after rows over the cutting down of trees, De Quincey's opium habits and his affair with a local girl who became pregnant. Wordsworth's attitude to the latter is a distinct case of the pot calling the kettle black, but William had the upper hand – De Quincey did not know about Annette and Caroline. De Quincey leaves us a vivid picture of Wordsworth as man as well as poet, one written before the final break. Wordsworth emerges as "not a well made man", with particularly unattractive legs. He skated like "a cow dancing a cotillion". He was self-centred, arrogant, lacked a good sense of humour. And yet he was adored by his women.

His desire to give full run to his talent meant that he swallowed his pride and asked the Lowther family, whom he had fought for years, for help. As a result he became Distributor of Stamps – a collector of stamp duty – for Westmoreland – with a salary that allowed him to live in modest comfort. In gratitude to the Lowther family he wrote some pretty awful odes about them and their estates, a fact that has been seized on by those who believe that the radical thinker had sold out. Wordsworth did, indeed, become a much tamer figure than he had been when young, but that is true of many people, and the fact that he bent the knee in order to continue the work that was his life while supporting the family he loved, is understandable, if not heroic.

In 1843, when Robert Southey died, Wordsworth became Poet Laureate. In 1847 his beloved daughter Dora died, an event which aged him. In 1850 he died at Rydal Mount after contracting pleurisy. Mary, having been told he was dying, decided that he too should be told. "William," she said, "you are going to Dora."

In the valley, during the long years of odd behaviour mellowing into gracious fame, Wordsworth became part of the furniture. All the anecdotes about him are gentle, suggesting that he was viewed with respect, even affection. One farmer, persuaded to a meeting to hear the Poet Laureate, was astonished to discover that it was old Wordsworth of Rydal.

The stories of his composing style were legion. He composed aloud as he walked, but it was a confined walk of a quarter or half a mile, between chosen limits. This he paced, up and down a cage of his own choosing. In general it appears the locals thought it possible that despite it all he had as much sense as anyone.

So many books have been written on Wordsworth's poetry, by so many eminent critics, that it seems irreverent to comment on it in a book such as this. But it is worth asking what it is that draws people by the hundred thousand to his houses and his grave, and that makes it necessary for the National Park to have a phone service for people who want to know if the daffodils are out in Dora's Field, or in Gowbarrow Park, Ullswater – the "lonely cloud" site.

Wordsworth deliberately chose to avoid high flown "poetic" language and to write his poems in the language of everyday life. His

work is therefore readily understandable. And its inspiration was almost always nature, to which he responded with passion. This passion is one shared to a greater or lesser degree by many people – and particularly by people who choose to visit Lakeland – his love is theirs, his philosophy appeals to them. And the fact that his enormous output includes some terrible verses is too human to be unforgiveable. ("Two voices are there. One is of the deep/The other of an old and silly sheep/And Wordsworth, both are thine . . " – The words are from a famous satire of 1891.)

Nor is it unforgiveable that, in addition to asking for help from the Lowthers, he also allowed his need for money to persuade him to write a series of anonymous scenic descriptions to accompany some etchings by a Norfolk vicar, the Rev. Joseph Wilkinson, even though he was aware that the etchings were not very good. This did not prevent the book from selling reasonably well, and many years later, in 1882, Wordsworth extended the descriptions and added a series of essays on landscape in general. These show the influence of the then current theories of "the Picturesque", although Wordsworth also used them to air personal prejudices. A pet hate of his was the white-washed cottage, which he thought spoilt a view almost beyond reprieve. Today a calendar of Lakeland scenes will almost always include at least one shot chosen for the presence of a white cottage: in two centuries that humble building has been transformed from being a blot on the landscape to being one of its most valued features.

Wordsworth's guide ran through several editions, and has recently been republished in paperback. It is a little schoolmasterish, but charming in spite of that, and well worth including on any list of Lakeland reading. Matthew Arnold told a nice story about it: apparently a clergyman once approached Wordsworth, bearing a copy of the guide, and asked politely whether Mr Wordsworth "had ever written anything else?"

When Wordsworth's funeral cortege was on its way from Rydal to Grasmere, a local observer remarked sadly that poets were no good when they were alive, but excellent when they died.

Wordsworth was not the first poet to appreciate the charms of the Grasmere valley. Thomas Grey glimpsed it from Dunmail Rise, and remarked that just beyond Helm Crag "opens one of the sweetest landscapes that art ever attempted to imitate". Gray also liked the church, a rude ecclesiastical edifice, appreciating the quiet dignity

Grasmere, from Loughrigg Terrace

which can be missed today, by those seeking the Wordsworth tombs and memorial. The church has an ancient festival, rushbearing, that links it to a time long before Gray, when the earth floor was rush-strewn for the comfort of the congregation. It was also, of course, unheated and the dales folk worshiped their god warmed by cloth from the wool of their Herdwick sheep. Every year the wool was replenished with the coming of summer, and a festival was held to renew the rush floor. Now every year, on the Saturday closest to 5 August, St Oswald's Day – the church is dedicated to him – children bring gifts, and receive the traditional payment, gingerbread.

Elsewhere the village is very much a tourist honey-pot, and is perhaps better visited in winter. But one link with its past is the continuance of the Grasmere sports, held annually on the nearest Thursday to 20 August, with traditional sports including fell racing and Cumberland/Westmoreland wrestling. The latter is worth watching if only for the costumes of the participants.

Those who have visited Grasmere village can continue around the lake to (334 064), or break out earlier onto the fells at (333 072), traversing below Silver How, keeping just above the woodland and avoiding Spedding Crag to meet the Elterwater road at (331 053).

The better view of Grasmere, indeed one of the finest of all lake views, is obtained by continuing along Loughrigg Terrace from our original route past Rydal Water.

Grasmere is unusual on its village side, the fields slipping quietly into the water. It is Wordsworth's lake "in a mountain urn". He saw its beauty, but recognised also that nature was impassive. He once recalled a pool on the stream from Grasmere, so quiet and lovely, and one day when a man came in search of his son he found him drowned in the pool.

I came to the terrace one evening and watched the sun fall over the mountain urn. A lone – and unusual – deer was startled into flight beyond the stone wall below the terrace. An owl kept me company as I walked back to Rydal. Of such things are poems made.

Our route follows the terrace to a beck, which is followed down to the lake. Go through the woodland at the lake edge, and then along the shore – of shingle, not grass, here. At the second boathouse the path – it is permissive rather than public from the wood to here – goes sharply left and up to the road at (335 063). Go right and then left at (334 064) for Hunting Stile and the fell near Hunting Stile Crag. A minor road is crossed (334 053) and the Langdale valley road, B5343, joined (332 049). Go left, then right to Elterwater.

The village is a small pretty place which once had a mill on Great Langdale Beck for the making of gunpowder.

From Elterwater the pathway, at (328 047), signed "Skelwith Bridge", along the Great Langdale Beck is followed. This is a superb pathway with fine views of the distinctive Langdale Pikes above the village. Of course the view is behind you all the way . . .

The river itself is also excellent, and Elterwater, when it appears from the tree cover, is equally good. It is the smallest of the lakes. Indeed it does not always appear on the list of lakes compiled by guide writers. It is also one of the more secret stretches of water since it is, relatively, isolated from roads and therefore more difficult of access. It is easy to find peace and quiet at Elterwater. Go early in the morning as the mist rises and you will be on your own, apart perhaps from a pair of red-breasted mergansers busily searching out their breakfast.

Skelwith Force is our last falls. It is not a great height of water, but

Elterwater village, and Langdale Pikes

Elterwater

it is a very long falls, a tumbling mass of white water. From the force we must follow lanes to return to Ambleside – first signed to Skelwith Fold, then to Ambleside. The walling here, at the roadside, is worth noting. The total Lakeland dry-stone walling must have used as many man-years of effort as the Great Wall of China . . . Well, almost.

Towards the end of the lane it runs close to the River Brathay with its inky-black pools above which there is the occasional white flash of a dipper. We join a larger road at Clappersgate. This was once a port for the slate and charcoal industries. Now the chief interest lies in the White Craggs Garden, a rock garden hewn from solid rock by the Hough family.

We cross the Brathay and join, for the last few yards, the main Langdale road. From here Ambleside is well seen and is a fitting end-point to our journey.

Distance

Round trip Rydal water, Grasmere and Elter Water –14km